DEDICATION

This book is dedicated to my husband, Greg, who, through his tenacity in overcoming life's challenges, has taught me to never give up. And to God, who, in His wisdom, inspired me to step out of my comfort zone and use the talents He gave me.

To God Be the Glory!

CATHIE

Cathie was too tired to move. Her head hurt, and her whole body ached. She felt like she had been hit by a truck. Her mind was confused. The pain she felt came from her head and her heart. Had it really happened, or had she just woken from a bad dream? It was a nightmare— an awful dream that seemed so real before she realized she had been asleep. Her thoughts are jumbled and confused as she wakens from her nightmare. She is confused about the condition of her clothes as well as about David and whether he really died. She lay there for a few more minutes, allowing her thoughts to clear.

David had been laid off for eleven months. Just when he felt ready to go back to work, the health issues started. Maybe it was stress from not working. Who knows? Their savings account had dwindled to nothing, and finances were tight. A recent renewal of their mortgage caused their payments to increase substantially due to high interest rates and, with three growing children, there was no excess cash. Their finances were in disarray.

She began to have some clarity. David had died suddenly and unexpectedly. How dare he leave her in such a mess! She frequently begged him, as things got tighter, to look at their finances and life insurance policies and see where they could cut expenses.

His recent involvement with gaming on his iPad was more important to him. An escape from the real world. His days were occupied with gaming. David felt he did a great job taking care of the kids when they weren't in school and looking after the house while she was at work. He did the laundry and cooked the meals, but every free moment he had was spent on his iPad. She often called his name more than once when she needed something, but he was so tuned into his games, he didn't hear her. His addiction was out of control.

She was proficient at staying on top of their finances, or so David thought. Then again, she always carried the financial burden. As long as there was money in the account when he went to the ATM, he thought all was well. He hadn't minded her taking over the finances after they were married. He was more than happy that she gave him his "allowance" every payday. It worked well for him. He didn't understand the stress she went through every time she paid a bill. If he didn't have to worry about money, then the worry didn't exist.

A nagging mole on his back caused him to book a doctor's appointment the previous month. The complete physical revealed not only the mole on his back but major discomfort in his spine and left leg. The mole was darker than his doctor felt comfortable with and had grown in size, according to David. To be on the safe side, Dr. Xtapa thought a biopsy was necessary. The mole was confirmed malignant, and a surgery date was booked. Dr. Xtapa didn't feel it was life threatening; however, when cancer was mentioned, David's fear crept in.

At the pre-op appointment, David and Cathie were advised he would be in hospital for only a day or two at the most. Hospitals were crowded, and patients didn't stay long. Most surgeries now were day procedures. With recent health care cuts, there were many changes that had become the new norm: staff shortages, supply shortages and, sometimes, lack of compassion. Nurses were run off their feet and overtime hours were expected. David was happy to be discharged the day after his surgery and recover in his own home—as long as surgery went well. When the oncology report came back, he would find out whether chemotherapy or radiation was necessary. Dr. Xtapa expected recovery time would be ten days. After a full recovery, David could begin a job search in his field of chemical engineering.

Layoffs came the previous year due to the economic downturn. It had been a tough year for the whole province of Alberta, but the industry started to pick up, and things were looking brighter. David was sure he would find work in the next month or so. He enjoyed his time off, but now it was time to get that second income back into the household.

His employment insurance was only seventy percent of his income, and it was due to run out in the next four weeks.

Cathie was hopeful he wouldn't have too much trouble finding a new job. Her dream of opening her own coaching business had been put on hold for over a year and, when David was laid off, she had had no choice but to return to her previous job as an insurance adjuster. They needed her income to keep the cashflow coming into the house. For several years prior to having children, she had worked in the insurance industry. She loved helping people and, although insurance was not an easy job, she was efficient, and her clients were grateful for her expertise. When she approached her previous manager about coming back to the company, they were grateful to have her back. Since her departure, the company had not succeeded in finding someone as suitable. She had an honourable work ethic, was capable, and was well-liked and respected by all the staff.

She liked her job, though it wasn't her dream job. She had a passion for coaching people and, in recent years, while the children were still at home, she found herself interested in self-help books and entrepreneurship. Always striving to be better, her dream now was to help other people find their passion in life. Like most people, she needed the guaranteed income and felt she had to settle with the insurance business until she and David got back on their feet financially.

Good things come to those who wait. She hoped it would be sooner rather than later.

David's surgery was scheduled for Thursday, and Cathie took him to the hospital that morning at eight a.m. She already had dropped their youngest daughter, Olivia, at daycare, and David Jr. and Anna were on their way to school on the school bus. David was ready to go when she arrived back at the house. He had been advised to wear loose clothing; once the surgery was finished, they would allow him to change into his own clothes. With all the cutbacks at the hospital, staff asked people to bring an extra change of clothes. Less clothing for the hospital staff to wash. David looked very casual in his checkered pyjama bottoms and black T-shirt. He was a tall, handsome man. His dark eyes and dark hair gave him an exotic look. Women turned their heads when they saw him in a mall or walking down the street. Cathie was so used to the head turns, she hardly noticed anymore.

The hospital was exceedingly busy when they arrived. Parking at the Foothills Hospital was usually a challenge but, this morning, they were lucky to find a parking spot quickly. After walking for ten minutes, they finally arrived inside, and the place was humming with activity. People came and went from every direction. The café was lined with people buying coffee before they headed to their jobs as nurses, doctors, or administrative staff. Those scheduled for day surgery attended the appropriate departments and waited in queue until called for their pre-surgery personal information. Cathie and David sat and waited patiently until David's name was called.

"Are you nervous?" she asked.

"Nope," David replied. "It's just a mole being removed and a little digging. No big deal."

He didn't want to alarm Cathie, but the pressure on his back was getting harder to tolerate. He was protecting her, or so he thought. They went through all the necessary protocols, and Cathie walked with David and the attending volunteer to the surgical ward. She kissed him goodbye and said she would pop back around twelve p.m., at which time he would be in the recovery room. David appeared nonchalant about the surgery, and Cathie wasn't overly concerned either. Dr. Xtapa had gone over everything with them, adding he was pretty sure there was nothing to be concerned about. He simply thought it was better to go in and remove the mole to put their minds at ease.

With a few hours of free time, Cathie returned to her office to review files. Usually she dressed in business attire, feeling a professionally dressed woman received more respect at work than one dressed casually. Today, since she would not be meeting with clients and only in the office for a few hours, she opted to wear her Diesel jeans and Tommy Hilfiger jean jacket. She still looked stylish in her red-wedged heels and matching red Coach purse. The red trim on her white T-shirt tied in perfectly. She had not done much shopping since David's layoff, but she always looked well put together. Her thick blonde hair was pulled back in a high ponytail. Just like her husband, heads turned when she walked by. She walked straight and tall and carried herself like a professional model. Her early morning workouts at home kept her body fit and slim.

She arrived at the office before the doors were open to clients, exchanged good-mornings with her coworkers, then grabbed a fresh coffee and headed to her office. Not a big coffee drinker, her secretary made sure to have a pot of McDonald's coffee brewing by the time Cathie arrived. That first cup was her favourite, and she loved the aroma of the arabica beans. She seldom made coffee at home, as David wasn't a coffee drinker, and the process was too much of a bother for just one cup.

She settled into her work and jumped when her phone rang—it was already eleven a.m. Seizing it from off her desk, she answered and was advised by Dr. Xtapa's assistant that he wanted to meet with her at the hospital. It didn't sound urgent, and she assumed David had come out of surgery earlier than planned and was asking for her. She expressed her thanks while closing her files and headed out the door.

It was a short drive to the hospital, but parking wasn't as easy this time and Cathie felt a little anxious as she hurried to the hospital entrance. When she finally reached the hospital's second floor, Unit 21, she was met by David's surgeon. The unit was hectic, with nurses moving quickly through the ward. These days, it was hard to know the difference between nursing and cleaning staff since they all dressed in scrubs.

Dr. Xtapa wore navy pants and blazer with a cream-coloured shirt. He was an elegant man in his mid-forties. He was from South Africa, tall, with blond hair. He spoke perfect English and had a gracious bedside manner.

"Mrs. Bryant, let's chat in here," he said, motioning to a side office where two nurses and the anaesthesiologist waited.

She was surprised to see the nurses.

"How's David?" she asked.

All eyes were on her.

"There were some complications," the anaesthesiologist said. "David had an allergic reaction to the anesthetic."

"Is he okay? I'd like to see him."

Dr. Xtapa spoke quietly. "I'm so sorry, Mrs. Bryant. David passed away forty minutes ago."

The room was enveloped in silence. She felt her eyes moving from one face to the next. *Did he say David had died forty minutes ago? That can't be right. Why are they all looking at me? Maybe I'm dreaming. No, this isn't real. I have to get back to work.*

The strong scent of smelling salts awakened her as Dr. Xtapa and a pretty blonde nurse attended to her. Her eyes focused on the name tag—Janice Jones, RN.

"What happened?" she asked.

"You fainted," Dr. Xtapa said.

It took a few seconds for Cathie to regain her bearings. David was gone. She was on her own with three children and a lifetime of memories.

Dr. Xtapa asked if she remembered what he had told her.

"Yes, but I don't understand." She was crying now and struggling to get the words out.

Nurse Janice handed her a glass of water.

"This was routine surgery," she said. "Four hours ago, my husband came in here a relatively healthy man. And now you're telling me he's dead?"

"Mrs. Bryant, David's heart stopped. We tried to revive him several times and were unsuccessful. Is there someone you would like us to call? You've had a bad shock."

"No," she replied. "I just want to go home and be with my children. May I see David before I leave?"

Nurse Janice gently laced her arm through Cathie's and led her to David. He had been moved into a room with a single bed. The curtains were open, and the sun shone brightly through the window. He looked peaceful lying in the bed, almost like he was taking a nap. His eyes were closed, and his dark hair was tousled as it usually was every morning. Janice brought Cathie a chair and gave her time to sit with David.

She held his hand, and tears streamed down her face. So many memories flooded her mind. They were supposed to grow old together. They had just talked about where they would like to travel when the kids were older and on their own. A river cruise in Norway. A trip to the east coast of Canada. A Mediterranean cruise.

We can plan our life as much as we want but, in the end, God makes the decisions.

This was the last time she would see her husband. All the frustrations of his being out of work, her responsibilities to pay the bills—it was all so trivial now. He was gone.

She kissed David goodbye and cried uncontrollably. Nurse Janice held her, speaking compassionately and once again asking if there were someone she might call.

Cathie declined her offer and, after thanking and embracing the kind nurse, she walked away. The nursing staff looked at her with sadness, acknowledging her pain. Was she emotionally stable enough to drive home? Cathie assured them she was fine, but she was simply going through the motions and not really comprehending what had happened. They told her the hospital would make arrangements for David's body to be taken to the funeral home, and the funeral home would contact her the following day.

As she left the hospital, she wondered how people could be laughing and smiling. Didn't they understand she had lost her husband? Now she had to go home and tell her children that Daddy was not coming home. *Why is life so unfair?*

The warm sun on her face did nothing to ease the pain in her heart. Sitting in her vehicle, her mind wandered back to the last conversation she had had with David that morning. Did she tell him she loved him? Did they hold hands or kiss? She couldn't remember. She wished she could turn the clock back and start the day over again. She sat for a few more minutes before turning the ignition. Glancing at the seat where David last sat, she saw his Tic Tacs. He had always loved Tic Tacs, but they weren't permitted in the hospital, as he could eat nothing prior to surgery. He had tossed them on the seat and reminded her to bring them when she came to see him. Simple things . . . now so important. Tears rolled down her face. She took a deep breath and tried to compose herself. It was almost two p.m., and the kids would be home by three-thirty.

Cathie called Susan, her best friend and neighbour, and asked her to pick up the children from school and Olivia from daycare.

"Something came up at work, and I won't be home until later tonight."

Susan was happy to help out. She and Alex, her husband, were not able to have a family and loved the Bryant children as their own. They were more like relatives than neighbours, and the children felt comfortable around them. Susan said she would bring them to her house and bring them back to Cathie's later.

Cathie thanked her but said nothing more about what had happened. She needed to do a few things before heading home.

Her first stop was the bank to check their account. Things looked bleak when she had checked online three days before. They had taken out a big mortgage on their dream home bought six years previously when the economy was booming. David's income as a chemical engineer provided more than enough for their family of five. But for the past twelve months, they had been living paycheque to paycheque. The economy had plummeted, and David had been laid off.

She entered the bank and went to the ATM. There was still a couple hundred dollars in the account that would keep her going for the next few days. She stopped at the front desk and chatted with the receptionist for a few minutes. Julie was pleasant, had a beautiful smile, and always dressed fashionably. As distraught as Cathie felt, she was composed as she asked Julie to see if they had taken out life insurance on their mortgage. The response was not favorable. There was no life insurance on their mortgage at this branch. She would have to check at home to see if David had taken it out elsewhere. Her head hurt, and it was hard to think. Julie reminded her about the next mortgage payment of $972.53 due in seven days. Cathie thanked her and headed back to her vehicle.

Now what? Where do I go? Who do I call? What do I do?

Their circle of friends had become small in the last few years. David originally had come from the east coast of Canada. His father had left his mother, older brother, and him when he was two years old. His mother had passed away a few years earlier and, with the family matriarch gone, he and his brother, Jim, lost contact. It had been several years since he or Cathie had spoken with Jim, a single man who led a very private life.

Cathie's parents had died many years previously as well. They were older when they had adopted Cathie and her sister, Lisa, from Vancouver, British Columbia. Cathy and Lisa lost touch over the years when Lisa's husband, Larry, caused problems over their parents' estate. Life had not been kind to Cathie in the past, and now she would have one more thing to deal with. Life problems were piling up. She got into her car and drove home, her mind a jumbled mess. *Where do I begin?*

She pulled into the driveway and opened the garage door. Everything was the same as when she had left that morning to drive David to the hospital. His golf clubs still sat by the foot of the stairs. How many times had she asked him to move them to the side so no one would trip over them? Anna had left her bike in the pathway of the stairs. Like father, like daughter. No semblance of order for either of them. The garage was a mess, but none of that mattered now. A day that began so routinely had taken a terrible twist. They had been married for fifteen years, and the "wow" in their marriage had worn off, replaced with the daily routine of life, but they still loved each other. She had laughed often with David and reminded him they were like an old pair of slippers—comfortable with each other. David would grin his silly grin and agree with her. Deep down, they truly loved each other, but life grew routine like everyone else's. Kids, jobs, house maintenance, bills. Their life was not like the fairytales often seen on television. Perfect home, perfect relationships, no worries. Now, she was on her own.

When she entered the house, the radio was playing country music, David's favourite. Breakfast dishes were still on the table. She went into auto-mode and made a cup of tea while loading the dishwasher, then called her office to advise she would be back the next morning. Moving to the couch, she stretched out and dozed off, soon dreaming of the past. She was twenty-one, standing at her parents' graveside and saying her final goodbyes. Following their accident, she had been forced to grow up quickly.

Cathie and Lisa had been adopted as babies. They were eleven months apart in age, born out of wedlock to Lois, a young girl who had spent most of her teenage years in trouble with the law. Lisa was the firstborn—a happy and beautiful dark-haired, brown-eyed baby that Lois tried her best to raise as a single parent. When she discovered she was pregnant a second time, her life situation had not improved. She struggled financially and emotionally, and the addition of a second child would be unfair to both. Social Services spent a lot of time working with Lois and, in the end, she made the difficult but wise decision to give up her babies.

Cathie was a newborn when she and Lisa were adopted, and each was the extreme opposite of the other. While Lisa was dark, Cathie had blonde hair and blue eyes. Both were beautiful children loved dearly by their parents, Robert and

Stephanie, who had tried for years to conceive. They were elated when Family Services informed them that two girls would be available for them to adopt, one eleven months old, and the second, a newborn. Although older than most first-time parents—Robert, forty-six, and Stephanie, forty-four—they were able to offer Cathie and Lisa the love and care they needed. The girls were a blessing, and their life was good.

It quickly ended one day when their car was broadsided by a semi-trailer, instantly killing their parents. It felt like yesterday, but here it was, nineteen years later, and Cathy now faced another tragedy. A widow at forty. Three children, no extra money, a huge mortgage, and David was gone.

Exhaustion and shock manipulated Cathie's dream. She and David were running through a busy city chased by thieves. They hid in an alley, holding their breath, waiting for the thieves to pass by. They tried to steal Cathie's purse, but David beat them off with a bat he had found in the alley. Breathing was difficult after frantic running. They did not speak, but David's eyes told her he would take care of her.

She woke up in a sweat; beads of perspiration dotted her forehead.

"David?" she called. "Where are you? I just had a horrible dream!"

That's strange. I wonder where he is. He was running to the store for just a few minutes.

She sat up. Her head hurt. She looked down at her clothes and felt more confused. *We're supposed to be going out tonight for drinks with Sam and Lynda.* She got up and looked around. *Where am I? Whose house is this?*

Her mind returned to the past. They had no children and lived in their apartment. Life was simple.

"I wonder what's taking David so long," she said aloud.

She got up and stumbled around, still disoriented. Nothing looked familiar. She lay down on the couch again and fell into a deep sleep.

A few hours later, she woke to her phone ringing.

"How are things?" Susan asked. "How is David doing? I put the kids to bed in my house since your place was dark, and I thought you might still be at the hospital.

Cathie began to cry.

"Cathie, what's wrong? I'm coming right over. Alex is here and can stay with the kids."

She stood up and found her way to the door. Walking past the mirror, she glanced at her reflection. Matted hair, smudged makeup, wrinkled clothing. What time was it anyway? It had been a long day and felt like forever since she had taken David to the hospital. Was it only this morning?

Susan knocked on the door and walked in. Cathie's dishevelled appearance startled her.

"What's going on?"

Cathie collapsed in Susan's arms. They had been friends since high school, and when Susan and Alex were married, they had purchased the house next door. Cathie and Susan were like sisters, there to support each other in any way they could. Leaning against her best friend was the emotional support she desperately needed.

Susan walked her to the kitchen and lowered her into a chair. She made tea and toast, certain Cathie hadn't eaten all day.

As they sat at the table, Cathie told her everything that had happened from the time she went to pick up David to the aftermath of her meeting with Dr. Xtapa and his medical team, then her visit to the bank. Her eyes filled with tears as she struggled to continue. Susan reached over and held her hands.

"Oh my God, Cathie! Why didn't you call and tell me right away? You've been alone all day with this?" She rose from her chair and wrapped her arms around her friend. They held each other and cried.

"How can I help you? When will you tell the children? *How* will you tell the children?"

Cathie sighed deeply before responding. "I don't know," she said between gulps and tears. "I just don't know. The hospital is arranging to have David's body taken to the funeral home today. Someone will call me in the morning to find out what arrangements I wish to make. David and I never discussed any of this. We thought we'd grow old together. There's so much to be done, and I just need to find my way through all this. I still can't believe this is happening to me. I know I'll get through it; I just don't know how."

Susan pulled her chair beside Cathie's and took her hand.

"We'll help you, and you won't have to do it alone."

After she had called Alex and relayed the events of the day, Susan spent the next few hours with Cathie. She would keep the children at her house until the next morning when they would be brought home for breakfast. She and Alex would be there to help Cathie and her family get through the coming days.

As the women sat and had tea, Cathie, between bouts of tears, recounted more of the day's events, especially her saying goodbye to David, her confused state of mind, and the bizarre dreams she had had after falling asleep on the couch.

Susan sat quietly and listened, feeling her friend's pain. Cathie confided her worries, her fears, her lack of money. David had been out of work for so long that the bills were now a concern.

"Where do I begin? This is all such a mess."

Susan suggested they begin with sleep, but Cathie's mind could not shut down long enough to sleep. She had too much to do. Who should she call first? Their families were small, and their circle of friends even smaller since David had been laid off. She had a few coworkers she casually saw outside of work, but David had lost all interest and contact with his former coworkers. She would talk to the funeral home tomorrow and put a notice in the paper. She also would call her office to let people know she would be off work for a while until she was able to put some of her affairs in order. Tomorrow was a new day, and she had to get through tonight first.

After chatting for a couple more hours, Susan again suggested they try to get some sleep. She had Ativan in her purse, which she had needed the previous week following a long dental appointment. She had been given four pills, but she had used only two. She offered one to Cathie.

"Here, take this," she said. "It will calm you down a bit and help you sleep. I know nothing will change, but we need you to get some rest so you can be there for your children in the morning."

Cathie willingly took the Ativan and, before long, it began to take effect. Susan had told her husband she would spend the night with Cathie, and both women prepared for bed.

Susan awoke at six a.m. and quietly went downstairs and made a pot of coffee. She then hurried to her house to check on the children, leaving a note for Cathie to call when she woke up. By the time Cathie woke, it was eight-thirty, and the children already had been fed breakfast. Susan told her she would bring them home at ten o'clock, which gave Cathie time to prepare her mind for how she would break the news to her children.

The next few weeks passed in a blur. How do you explain to children that their father has died? What do you share with them while uncertain about your own beliefs?

Susan took the children again when Cathie went out on her own to do some needed clothes shopping for them and for herself. There were a few difficult moments when the friendly salesclerk complimented her choice of an especially flattering navy-blue dress. When she asked, "What's the special occasion?" Cathie fell apart. The clerk could only offer sympathies without knowing what else to say.

Rather than wearing traditional black, Cathie thought it more appropriate to wear navy. Anna and Olivia would look sweet in navy skirts and white sailor blouses. David Jr. would look so grown up in his navy pants, white shirt, and navy-striped tie. He would now be the man of the house, filling his dad's footsteps. The road ahead would be difficult for them all.

~

The day of the funeral was hard. The children clung to Cathie. As neither she nor David had any relatives, Susan and Alex were their family. The children thought of them as their aunt and uncle. They both stood with Cathie and the children and were there to hold them when it was more than they could bear. There were more people at the funeral than Cathie could have imagined. Old friends from high school, previous coworkers, David's and her current coworkers, parents of her children's friends. She felt deeply grateful to have so much love and support.

The minister spoke many kind words about David and his marriage to Cathie as well as the beautiful family they had made together. Soon after the reception lunch, the minister stopped by to chat with Cathie and promised to check in on her and the children in the coming weeks.

When two weeks had passed, Cathie still felt she was living in a fog. The children didn't understand where their father was. They knew nothing of death or heaven or anything remotely related to either. Neither Cathie nor David had been raised with any church connection, and they never questioned anything about eternity or an afterlife. Like many people, they lived for today—work, school, children, bills, and everything in between. Cathie dabbled in Buddhism in her younger years, but it wasn't her cup of tea. David was a self-proclaimed agnostic. He wasn't sure what he believed in and would never be caught up in religion or spirituality. In no way would he teach anything on the topic to his children. "Let them find their own way," he often said. That's how his parents raised him, and he had turned out pretty well.

Cathie had to make the decision about whether or not to cremate David. Should they have a burial plot the children could visit? She was grateful for the minister's guidance. He suggested cremation and thought it best to have David buried in a cemetery where Cathie and the children could visit at any time. All of this was very new to Cathie, as her parents had been cremated and their ashes sprinkled on the shores of Vancouver. At the time of their parents' passing, Cathie and her sister knew they would not be returning to Vancouver. A burial plot, therefore, was not important to them.

In the days after the funeral, she made arrangements, through the employee-assistance program at work, for grief counselling for herself and her children. David Jr. and Anna were back in school. Cathie contacted their teachers to advise of David's passing, and the teachers were well versed in handling parental deaths. The children moved through each day and, like most, were fairly resilient. They often asked about David, and Cathie never kept anything from them. They regularly talked about their father. Olivia asked where Daddy was and, since Cathie didn't know how to respond, she told her that Daddy is in heaven with the angels. That's what the minister said at the funeral, and it seemed to pacify Olivia and her siblings.

With the funeral behind them, Cathie started delving into financial affairs. The bank staff were compassionate and helpful, instructing her to have bills forwarded to them for their estate department to handle. She went to the bank a second time shortly after David's passing and was grateful for the financial advisor they assigned to her. Stephen MacPherson was a few years older than Cathie. He was quiet, compassionate, and treated her with kindness.

"The bank will be here for you," he said.

True to his word, he delayed her loan and mortgage payments for three weeks.

An appointment had been set up for ten a.m., and she looked stylish in her navy dress and slingback navy shoes. As she glanced at herself in the mirror, her tired eyes looked back at her. She applied makeup and covered the dark circles. She hadn't been sleeping well, and all she really wanted to do was crawl back into bed and pull the covers over her. She dreaded the bank appointment. Everything was all too real now, all her responsibility. Today, she would find out exactly where she financially stood.

~

She arrived at the bank a few minutes before her appointment time. Several items needed to go into the safe-deposit box, but Stephen was waiting for her when she arrived. He greeted her warmly in the reception area, and she followed him into his office. He asked how she and the children were doing and again expressed his sympathies. After a fleeting exchange of pleasantries, the hammer hit. Things were far worse than she had thought. The mortgage payment would be due the next week, the truck payment the following week, and the car payment the week after that. How in

God's name could she manage this? She was sure that life insurance had been taken out on their loans at one time or another, but David eventually had to cancel the policies on the house and the vehicles. There were so many monthly payments that she never even noticed the cancellations.

She sobbed uncontrollably as Stephen handed her Kleenex after Kleenex. His hands were tied. He could waive a couple of mortgage and loan payments but, eventually, the bank would want the money. Her head throbbed. She needed money. She needed to sell the house. She needed someone to come and take care of her.

Stephen kindly asked if she would like a cup of coffee or tea, and she gratefully nodded in response. He brought her tea in a large mug then started going through her financial records. He would go to bat for her, but she would have to bring him all financial information from outside the bank in the coming days so that he could see what he might do to help her. The house had to be sold, and she could then reapply for a smaller mortgage on a smaller property. This would provide her with a more manageable payment arrangement. David's truck could be sold and the proceeds applied to the loan, thereby eliminating one loan payment. In addition, she was willing to sell her Nissan Murano and buy a smaller, cheaper vehicle, eliminating another payment. The only thing left would be the mortgage and the expense of raising three children. Stephen helped her see the overall picture in a clearer and more manageable way.

After much discussion about loans and mortgages, he accompanied her to the safe-deposit box to get the Will. Cathie told him they had had their Wills completed three years before, shortly after Olivia, their last child, was born. When David's Will was retrieved from the box, she was surprised to find an envelope marked "Confidential" in David's handwriting underneath the folder. She opened it when they returned to Stephen's office. He watched as she read the contents and saw her face become gray. She slumped against the back of the chair.

"What's wrong?" he asked.

Once again, Cathie's tears flowed. "Oh my God . . . David fathered a child from an affair he had!"

A photograph fell out of the envelope—a boy, around five years old, who resembled David Jr. "Tyler" was the name on the back of the photo. There were also papers revealing the agreement David had signed, stating he would pay child support to the boy's mother.

Cathie felt blindsided. *Will this nightmare never end? Now what?*

She tried hard to compose herself, and Stephen patiently waited. She looked up from what she had been reading.

"I can get through this," she said.

She stood up and thanked Stephen for his help. "I don't know how this will all work out, but I know it will."

He made an appointment for her to return the following week. Meanwhile, he would arrange with the bank to delay the payments until she checked with the car dealership about turning in both vehicles and purchasing a smaller, more efficient car.

As she walked out of the bank, the cool air stroked her face. She looked confident and sophisticated in her elegant dress and heels as she approached her Murano. Inside the car, she put her head on the steering wheel and silently spoke to the universe.

I don't know if anyone can hear me, but I need some help. God, if you truly are there, please help me. I can't do this alone.

Feeling more composed, she made her way to the dealership. There was nothing to rush home to now. David Jr. and Anna were in school for another few hours, and Olivia was at daycare. Cathie was grateful for Denise, her daycare provider, who had become more of a friend in the few weeks since David's passing.

Cathie stopped at the Tim Hortons drive-thru and ordered a Double Double before she went to the Nissan dealership. As much as she loved her Murano, now was as good a time as any to make some changes in her life, and finances were her top priority.

Just before pulling into the dealership, she put a smile on her face and made a conscious effort to get through the next hour. Coffee in hand, she walked through the front door and was cheerily greeted by Danica, the receptionist.

"Good morning! How may I help you?"

"Good morning," Cathie replied. "May I speak with one of your salesmen regarding a purchase and a trade?"

"Absolutely!" Danica said enthusiastically. "May I have your name, and I'll see who is available."

"Cathie Bryant—my husband and I purchased a vehicle here about a year ago. You may have a record of who assisted us. I think his name was Scott."

"Scott no longer works here, Mrs. Bryant. Let me see who else is available. If you'd take a seat for a moment, I'll have someone with you shortly."

Cathie was grateful when she saw a mature gentleman walking toward her with his hand extended.

"Hi, Mrs. Bryant. My name is Conrad Jamieson, and I would be happy to assist you. Let's go into my office and have a chat."

He led her into his office and offered her a chair then seated himself behind his desk. He reached for a pen and began writing. His questions were easy enough to answer, and he wrote what she said in a notepad. He was a kind man and an attentive listener.

She explained her situation, saying her first priority was selling her husband's truck and trading her Murano for something smaller. Conrad's manner was sympathetic to the tragic loss of her husband at a young age. He felt compassion for her and wanted to help however he could. Still, he had to make it clear she would take a huge loss by trading in both vehicles. As he spoke, he saw the panic in her eyes.

"We'll figure something out, Cathie," he said encouragingly. "I'm here to help you."

He wrote the details of David's truck, a newer model Nissan Titan, burgundy in colour with low mileage. It would be high in demand, and he was sure he would find a buyer.

Cathie added she wasn't overly concerned about making a profit and simply wanted to get rid of the loan. After a few more questions and details, they left his office and went outside to see the Murano. It was a fine vehicle, well maintained, fully equipped with all the bells and whistles. With the shortage of used vehicles in the past few months,

Conrad was more confident in finding a buyer now that he had seen the condition of the car, especially the leather seats and command start.

When they returned to his office, he gave her his business card and said he would contact her in a couple of days to let her know whatever information he had.

She left the dealership, feeling slightly more hopeful. One day at a time, one step at a time, one moment at a time.

With all that had happened, she had not taken time to deal with her grief. She required not only financial assistance but also emotional help. At Susan's suggestion, she contacted her supervisor who referred her to the employee assistance program through the insurance company. It was recommended she take at least six weeks off work and attend bi-weekly Zoom sessions with a qualified professional. The time away from her job meant quality time with her children and would allow her to tie up all the loose ends of her life. Mentally making notes, she thought about the photograph and the information she had discovered in the safe-deposit box. That would have to be dealt with at a later date.

As she drove down a familiar street, she noticed a sign on the local Catholic Church: *When life feels as if it is crashing down, look up! God has his hands on you.*

Sure, God. If you only knew!

She continued to drive without realizing she had driven to the older part of Calgary's Bowness area. This was where she and David had lived when they were first married. She parked the car, got out, and walked toward the park at the end of the street. The sun shone brightly and, although it was June, it was cooler than normal. The winds blew, and she wrapped her scarf more tightly around her neck. She proceeded to the swings, chose one, and began rocking back and forth. The motion relaxed her, and she closed her eyes as she tightly held on to the bars. No one was in the park, and she let her mind wander back to 2004.

She had left an abusive relationship twelve months earlier and was single now, living on her own. For five months on and off, she had been casually dating Devon but, recently, she noticed some very erratic behaviours. His consideration and kindnesses had impressed her when they were first together. He was always a gentleman, opening doors and pulling out chairs for her. During the following few weeks, though, he appeared tense and agitated, not wanting her to go anywhere without his knowing where she was and whom she was with. He constantly nagged her, and she had felt increasingly uncomfortable. On several occasions, when his temper flared and she walked away, he roughly grabbed her arm or her hair. Domestic violence was something she had seen and learned about on television ads and, while this was new behaviour for Devon, she was aware it was not only unacceptable but dangerous.

The day came when she knew she was in trouble. They had planned a special evening of dinner and dancing. She took extra care to look her best and was pleased with the red dress she had purchased that day. Devon arrived at six p.m. and let himself in just as she walked out of her bedroom. His hair was disheveled and his mood as dark as the scowl on his face. He looked handsome in his black suede jacket, pink Hermes shirt and denim pants, but his demeanor was off. Without greeting her, he snidely commented about her dress.

"Don't you think it's a little too short? You look like a hooker!"

As he walked past her, she could smell whiskey on his breath, but the more she tried to lighten the atmosphere, the more agitated he became.

"Devon!" she finally said, "Tonight doesn't seem to be the best of nights to go out for dinner. You aren't your happy self. Why don't we try again tomorrow? I think maybe you should head home, and we can chat in the morning."

Her words angered him, and he started badgering and taunting her, accusing her of no longer loving him. She must be seeing someone else. Why would she dress so sleazily when she was going out with him? She had another man already, didn't she? Did she need to look so sexy to attract someone else?

She denied his accusations, but he would not let up. Continuing to throw insults at her, she demanded that he leave. The combination of alcohol, anger, and now feeling rejection was too much for him.

He took his first swing at her, but she moved quickly enough to avoid his fist. The second time she was not as lucky. He caught her by surprise, hitting her left cheek and knocking her to the floor. Droplets of blood oozed from her cheek, but he was not finished with her. His insults continued, then he took a third swing, aiming for her face. She again moved quickly and was able to roll. Devon hit the floor with a thud as her heart pounded. Her face hurt, and she could feel blood dripping from the open wound.

Still, she had her wits about her and, thinking fast, she grabbed the lamp off the end table and smashed it on his head as hard as she could. God was on her side. Surprised at her own strength, the force of her action had knocked Devon unconscious. She jumped up and ran for the door. As Devon lay semi-conscious, she ran screaming to her next-door neighbour, despite their only having exchanged occasional greetings. His name was David, and she banged on his door, which he opened almost instantly. She pushed her way inside and shut the door.

"My boyfriend is drunk and he's beating me up . . . I'm afraid he's going to kill me!"

David grabbed his cell phone and called 911. He gave his townhouse address and described as much of the incident as Cathie had told him, stating the assailant was next door and semi-conscious. They waited for the RCMP, and David tried to calm her. Her red dress was torn, her hair pulled from the updo she had styled, and blood still ran down her cheek. He locked the front door and went to find a clean warm facecloth. Sitting on the couch, waiting for the police, she told him more of what happened.

The RCMP seemed to take forever. Her heart continued to race, and she nervously stood and paced back and forth then sat again. She was fearful Devon would break into her neighbour's house. David looked out the window, watching for the police. When two RCMP officers arrived, he narrowly opened the door to let them in. Their first concern was to ensure Cathie was all right and, despite the blood on her face, not in need of emergency medical assistance.

After several minutes of questioning, the officers went to Cathie's house. Devon was regaining consciousness, and they found him dazed and bleeding from the blow to his head. They called for back-up, and he was taken away in handcuffs. Two officers remained with Cathie and David, taking statements from them. Cathie looked bedraggled, but beneath her messy hair, torn dress, and bruised eye and cheek, David saw how beautiful she was.

The officers asked her if she wished to press charges. Domestic violence was on the rise, they said. Once the case was reviewed, the officers would be able to lay charges against Devon without Cathie's consent. However, on their recommendation, she laid charges against him.

They also provided her with contact information for the sexual-assault division. There she would find a support professional to help her deal with post-traumatic emotions. After the officers left, David stayed for a while, and they sat and chatted after he helped her clean up the broken lamp. Though he didn't ask any more questions, Cathie was sure he was curious. After all, she had been dressed like she was going somewhere special, and her red dress didn't hide her curvy body. Her long, blonde hair had been pulled back into a bun, and a few strands now flowed freely on her face and down her back.

They chatted a while longer and, after assuring him she was all right, she thanked him again.

"Thanks so much for being here for me. I don't know what might have happened had you not been home." she said.

When he left, she called the Sexual Assault Centre. Her case was nonsexual, but speaking with a professional would be of benefit. She was unsure whether she would suffer any trauma and was grateful for the assistance made available.

The next day, one of the officers called to let her know the date of Devon's court appearance. He had been arrested, charged, and incarcerated. A restraining order would be issued prohibiting him from contacting Cathie.

~

The sound of children on the playground jarred Cathie back to reality. She shivered, though she wasn't cold. Memories of Devon were a thing of the past, but this was how David came into her life. Now she wanted to get home, start supper, and pick up Olivia from daycare before David Jr. and Anna's school bus dropped them off.

Early in the next week, she received good news from Conrad at the car dealership.

"How are you, Mrs. Bryant? I think I have a buyer for your husband's truck, and there's a good possibility I have buyer for your Murano. Would you be able to bring the truck in on Friday at two o'clock?"

"Absolutely!" Cathie replied.

Through the remainder of the week, she occupied her time going through David's clothing and belongings. This was easier to do while the children were in school. She sat on the bed in her Lululemon leggings and top. There was no need to dress up these days. She didn't leave the house often.

She picked up one of David's favourite cashmere sweaters and held it close to her face. It was baby blue, and she remembered how intensely blue his eyes looked when he wore it. As she held it close to her nose, his scent was unmistakable. She saw his smile and felt his presence. It was still hard to believe he was gone. Deep in memories, she was startled to hear her name.

"Cathie, are you upstairs?"

"Yes, come on up!" she replied.

Susan dropped by often with meals, coffee, and wine. How would Cathie ever repay her? As Susan walked into the bedroom, she carried a tray with a thermos of hot coffee, two mugs, a small bottle of Bailey's Irish Cream, and a plate of muffins and cheese. Cathie wasn't eating much these days, and meals had been left at the house for her and the children from staff at the insurance company and caring neighbours. She made sure the children ate, but she seldom felt hungry. Nonetheless, there were times when her stomach growled loudly, reminding her she hadn't eaten. Her mind was more focused on whatever had to be dealt with next.

There were so many people to thank: those who had come to the funeral, those who had sent cards and flowers, those who had left meals. She had many cards of thanks to write, but that was for another day.

Susan and Cathie enjoyed muffins and a quick coffee before going through David's personal items. There were lots of tears and laughter. Cathie was grateful she didn't have to sort through all this alone.

The day felt as if David had been gone forever. Was it really only three weeks? The children continued to adjust to life without their father; however, Cathie missed him terribly. The daytime hours passed quickly, as there was much to do: taking care of his affairs, cleaning out his closets and drawers, and, of course, taking the children to school and daycare and preparing meals. An extra set of hands really did make a difference.

The week had passed quickly when Friday came, and Cathie headed to the dealership with David's truck. She smiled to herself, recalling how much pride he had taken in his truck. He was obsessed with it, always cleaning, polishing, and vacuuming. There wasn't much to clean out now except the glove box. She wanted to be certain all the necessary manuals were available. While checking for the registration, she found an envelope with receipts filed in numerical order and signed by Laura Jayne Comerford. There were seven receipts in total all made payable to David Bryant for $800 a month. The memo said, "child support for Tyler Comerford."

The other woman and child in David's life now had names. How long had these payments been going on? Why hadn't David shared any of this with her? How she longed to hear the story. There were so many questions she wished she could ask him, but she needed to refocus on getting the truck to the dealership today.

Arriving promptly at two p.m., Conrad was waiting for her. The reception area was well lit with many windows, and the sun shone brightly on the new vehicles. The friendly receptionist greeted Cathie with a smile, and Conrad welcomed her warmly. She appeared to be doing better today then when he had seen her last. He offered her coffee, and they went to his office.

Conrad was excited to tell her about the potential buyer, although nothing would be confirmed until the buyer checked out the truck. If all went well, he hoped to sell it and have an extra $5000 left over for Cathie once the loan was paid off. As he shared details, he saw the relief in her eyes and the smile on her face.

He again mentioned the possibility of having a buyer for her. He had been on the lookout for a good used vehicle for her—one that was reliable, in good condition, and fell within her budget. She had told him she wanted low or no monthly payments, and he worked hard to make this happen, dispelling the pushy car salesman stereotype. He cared about his clients.

For Cathie, he reminded her of her father—kind, gentle, and caring. She felt at ease dealing with him, and now she felt she had found a new friend.

By the end of the day, the truck was sold. Conrad had been able to add an extra $1000 to the price and both buyer and seller were happy with the deal. When the paperwork had been signed, he gave Cathie a ride home so that she could pick up her Murano and collect Olivia from daycare. They shook hands, and Conrad reassured her everything would work out for her. Cathie felt relieved and grateful for his kindness.

She slowly adjusted to her new life though still had a long road ahead of her. Today, however, was a good day, and she felt a little more at peace. Tomorrow she would go to the bank and happily pay off David's truck loan.

LAURA COMERFORD

The third day of the month was another busy workday, and Laura was exhausted. All she wanted to do was pick up her son from daycare and get home to a warm bath and a good book after Tyler's bedtime.

The other children had been picked up by the time she arrived, and Tyler was playing with Barbara's children, Troy and Jessica. While Laura collected Tyler's jacket and backpack, Barbara mentioned that the cheque Laura had given her for the month had been returned. Laura looked up in surprise.

"That can't be possible," she said. "The money is in the account."

She hadn't spoken with David personally for the past two years, but his child-support payments were like clockwork.

Every month for the past five years, on the twenty-ninth of the month, funds were deposited into her account.

Six years before, she and David had had a brief affair while in Calgary attending a training course for their jobs. David lived in Calgary, and Laura was from Saskatoon. They met on the first day of their course, sitting beside each other at the opening training session. Laura was blonde, petite, and a few years younger than David. She was shy, insecure, and new to her role as a chemical engineer. David had been an engineer for a few years and familiar with being on course. He had attended several in the past few years and, although he lived in Calgary, he was required to stay in the host hotel given the intense training schedule.

He had taken a seat beside Laura and struck up a friendly conversation while waiting for the instructor to begin. They exchanged small talk, saying where they were from and how long they had been engineers. When the instructor began speaking, they focused on what they would learn in the coming days.

David didn't know anyone else in the course, and when lunch time rolled around, he asked Laura if she would have a quick lunch with him at the hotel restaurant. She appreciated his friendliness and saw no harm in their having lunch together. Young and single, she enjoyed the attention, and David was intrigued by this young woman.

His recent marital challenges had left him feeling isolated while his wife was wholly consumed with caring for their one-year-old son.

By the third day, Laura and David spent breaks and lunches together. The attendee numbers were large, and there was neither interest in nor attention paid to the newly connected couple. Laura was smitten with David's attention, and David felt the same. By the fourth evening, they had spent a romantic evening together. After a few glasses of wine, David returned to Laura's room where they shared a night of passion. That single magical evening produced more than beautiful memories. Nine months later, Tyler was born. One night not only resulted in a new life but major stresses and financial challenges for both David and Laura.

David already had a wife and a child at home, and he realized his mistake the next day. It had been casual sex, and he and Laura parted on good terms. He would go home and rekindle his life with his wife, making a vow nothing like this would ever happen again. And it never did.

He had been shocked when Laura contacted him nine months later to tell him her news. At first, he tried to deny the baby was his, but when Laura shared the dates and sent David a photo of the new baby boy, denial was not an option. David never shared his infidelity with Cathie. Eventually, their marriage was revived and they now expected their second baby. A third child would arrive a few years later.

Laura remained a single parent and, for the last five years, she raised Tyler on her own. Monthly, she received a cheque from David; in return, she sent him receipts. She also sent him the occasional photo of Tyler via the intranet at work. No one would ever know their secret.

Although laid off, David continued to make his monthly payments to Laura through a bank account he held in his own name at a different bank. He had received a severance package but told Cathie he received only a portion of the full amount. His secret remained safe. Cathie was none the wiser, and everything had worked out well. That is, until he died.

~

Laura apologized to Barbara. She felt embarrassed, having prided herself on keeping her finances in order. She was furious with David and felt her blood pressure rise dramatically, leaving her red in the face. She would send him a not-so-pleasant email; meanwhile, she had to get Tyler home, fed, and bathed. Being a single mother was not easy, but she cherished every moment with her little man. She felt God had blessed her. There were struggles, but she had strong support from her parents and two sisters. He had been born out of wedlock, but when her parents had seen their grandson, all was right in their world. They had never met David nor cared to. They simply knew he faithfully contributed monthly to Laura's account for Tyler's support, and they were grateful for that much.

Later that evening, after Tyler was tucked into bed, Laura sent an email to David at work. Part of their agreement was contact by email or snail mail. No texts or phone calls. They never involved a lawyer with the custody agreement, as they did not think it necessary. Until today, things had worked well. Laura sent pictures and infrequent updates on Tyler. Aside from monthly child support, David sent extras for Christmas and birthdays. He faithfully kept his part of the deal in the five years since Tyler's birth and, in return, Laura did the same. Tyler never knew who his father was, and he never asked. He was surrounded by the love of his mother, his grandparents, and his aunties.

Laura was exhausted by the time she finished the email and prepared her clothes and lunch for the following day. Her evenings with Tyler were always rewarding but, after a full day of work, her bed was always a sweet refuge. Big pillows, soft down duvet. Luxury at its finest. Most times, she was sound asleep within minutes of her head resting on her pillow.

She handled money shrewdly and had tucked away some of what David had given her. Later the next day, she paid Barbara in cash and once again apologized. Still angry at David's not having paid her properly, she was further enraged that evening to find her email had bounced back. What the hell was he doing? They had an arrangement, and she always held up her end of the bargain. Tomorrow she would break the rules and call his office. Embarrassment and frustration were taking their toll.

The following morning, settled in her office behind closed doors, she called David's office and was shocked to learn "David Bryant no longer works at this firm." She understood employee confidentiality, but she nevertheless would ask.

"How long ago did he leave? We used to be coworkers, and I'm trying to locate him," she told the receptionist.

"Over a year ago," the receptionist replied, ignoring confidentiality. "Obviously, you haven't heard. I'm sorry to tell you that David recently passed away."

Laura was stunned. "Oh no!" she said.

She was dumbfounded, not so much for the personal loss but more for his family and—of course—for the financial strain now created for her. She quickly offered her condolences and thanked the receptionist for letting her know. A long time passed before Laura moved from her desk. This was going to change everything.

CATHIE

With David's truck loan paid off, Cathie's finances looked more manageable. The bank had been helpful during the past six weeks, and she was thankful for their guidance. Her bereavement leave from work would end the following week, and she felt almost ready to return to her job. During the last week, she finally had found time to grieve the loss of David. Sadness, anger, loss—raw emotions. Some days, she felt as if she were on a rollercoaster. Weekly counselling helped and, week by week, she discovered her inner strength. She missed David terribly but knew her focus now was their three children. Her counsellor advised her to start journalling her thoughts and feelings on paper and, although this was new to Cathie, she found it helpful. Susan was still her ideal support, and Cathie knew she would get through this just as she had other life challenges.

Together over a glass of wine one night, Cathie confided to Susan more intimate details of the financial difficulties she and David had had prior to his death. It was also a good time to tell her about the paperwork she had found in the safe-deposit box. Susan's mouth opened wide in disbelief. On the outside, life at the Bryant household had looked normal: a beautiful home, two new vehicles, well-behaved children.

Susan asked how things were for her now that David's truck had sold.

"Some of the pressure has been relieved," Cathie said, "but there is still work to do on selling the Murano and finding a smaller car. I'll also have to look at selling the house. I don't want to leave the neighbourhood, and you especially, but I have to look at the financial strain this house will create. And I'm not sure what to do about this other child."

She still was living with the shock of David's affair and confused about how she should handle it. No decisions were made that night, but it felt good to share some of her burdens with her good friend.

LAURA

What would she do now? David was gone, but her greater loss was the income he had provided for Tyler. Eight hundred dollars a month was not a lot of money for some people but, to a single mother, it was a fortune. Her soft heart made her think of David's wife and children. She didn't know anything about them other than that he had a family now mourning his loss. The fact he was a married man was not important to her when they had spent five days and an evening of passion together six years earlier. She had been young and lonely at the time. She learned the hard way that a moment of not thinking clearly could change the trajectory of life. How many lives were affected in the heat of passion? Thank God that was all in the past. She never regretted the birth of her son, but she sometimes carried the guilt of the financial burden this must have placed on David's family.

Had he ever shared with his wife that he had another son? How did she react? Did his children know they had a half-brother? She would never know. David was gone, and she had no way to track down his family.

DAVID JR.

Years had passed since his dad died. He was eighteen years old. He was finally on his own ready to start his new life. He had packed his car and driven for six hours to Saskatoon from Calgary. Driving his red Honda S2000, people still turned their heads when they saw the flashy vehicle on the highway. Sometimes, it was young girls who were attracted but, more often than not, it was the thirty year old men who would have given anything to have a super-charged car like this one.

David had started working at Carnival Cinemas when he was fourteen years old. He wasn't much of a spender, so every dollar he earned he put in his bank account. Only a few months before high school ended, his mother co-signed a loan for him to purchase his dream vehicle. The hours he spent checking Buy-and-Sell sites had paid off after inquiring about the price and finding it within his budget. With a large down payment, the vehicle was his after two weeks. He smiled remembering the first time driving it to school, and now, here he was on the highway, revving up his engine and enjoying the drive.

The sun shone brightly, and the prairie roads were straight and dry. There were combines and semi-trucks in the fields taking off the ripened grain and canola. Lots of dust on the prairie side roads. This was the life!

It was hard leaving his mother and two younger sisters, Anna now sixteen, and Olivia, thirteen. He had become the man of the house twelve years earlier when his dad suddenly passed away. He still had happy memories of his father: playing cars and trucks when he was five or six, throwing a football in the backyard. His father had taught him to skate when he was four, but his favourite memory was riding in his father's new truck and going for ice cream. This was a memory he would hold on to forever. It was one of the last times he had seen his father. He loved spending time with him, and they had had a great relationship. He was only six when his father died, but his mother had treated him as if he were much older and, as the years passed, David Jr. took on more responsibility than most teenagers. He was a well-mannered young man and being forced to grow up quickly had served him well.

Being a star athlete in basketball and receiving honors all through high school earned him a basketball scholarship at the University of Saskatchewan. He would major in Human Resources and was excited to see where the future would take him. He was close to his mother and, although sad to leave her and his sisters, he was excited for the coming year. He sang loudly with the radio and felt how good his life was. This would be his year to experience life on his own, to spread his wings and fly. He would meet two of his high-school buddies in Saskatoon in a couple of days. They had rented a place of their own—no parents, no rules. Life couldn't get any better than this.

CATHIE

As her first-born son pulled out of the driveway in his red convertible, Cathie and her girls wiped away their tears. Where had the years gone? David Jr., her rock, was leaving home. She had become dependent on him, and he had stepped up to the role of man of the house. He was responsible at a young age and, as he grew older, he took his role seriously. She was proud of her son. He had turned out to be a great kid, and now he was off to Saskatoon to begin a new venture. She knew he had a great future ahead of him.

The first few years after David passed were the hardest. She had been able to sell her Murano along with David's truck, pay off loans, and downsize her home. She found the perfect house for her family and felt blessed when she learned she had a $50,000 life-insurance policy on David through her benefits at the insurance company. This allowed her to move into a home more financially manageable. She was sad to leave the neighbourhood she loved, and leave her best friend, but having minimal debt and being able to provide for her family was more important. Her relationship with Susan continued over the years, and they made sure to get together on a regular basis a couple of times a month.

It took some time to settle into a new normal. There were always challenges being a single mother and working full time. Day care, school, sick kids, school concerts, etc. Cathie's employer was accommodating when it came to family, and she was careful to never take advantage of the kindnesses shown to her.

After a few years had passed, she was offered a senior management position. Her new six-figure income provided her the means to live a more luxurious life. She was thankful she no longer needed to struggle financially and wanted never to deal with financial stress again.

Even with a higher income, Cathie's life remained simple and without fanfare. Family activities, work, and working out at the gym kept her schedule full. She enjoyed an occasional date and her get-togethers with Susan. In time, new friendships at work were formed and, once or twice each month, the women would gather for a fun evening. Her life was full, easy, and, for the most part, stress free. Now that David Jr. had moved to Saskatoon, things would change, as she would take occasional trips to visit him.

LAURA

After Laura learned of David's passing, she checked the online obituaries in the *Calgary Herald*. Sometimes a death notice revealed the cause of death, and this was of concern for her son. Illnesses often are hereditary, and she wanted to be informed for the future. She found David's obituary and learned he had died suddenly of complications during surgery. Left to mourn, his loving wife, Cathie and three children, David Jr., six years old, Anna, four years old, and baby Olivia, one year old.

Her eyes filled with tears as she read. How difficult to tragically lose a husband and father. She felt especially thankful to have Tyler from the brief affair. She was unsure how she would financially manage going forward, but she would not pursue going after David's estate. His family already had enough to deal with. She would inform her parents of David's passing and was confident they would help her when necessary. As life happens, six months later, she was promoted to a supervisory role at work, and the pay increase more than covered the monthly eight hundred dollars.

She wanted to send a sympathy card to Cathie and her family but decided against doing so. Why open a door that had been long closed? She also knew the time would come when she would share the information about Tyler's father, but not until Tyler was much older.

Laura's life moved on and, when Tyler was seven years old, she met Jonathan Winters. They had been set up on a dinner date by mutual friends. Laura's friend and co worker, Andrea, thought Jonathan and Laura would be well suited, though it took much convincing. On the night of the arranged dinner, Andrea and her husband, Cal, picked Laura up at her home. When she came out the front door, Cal let out a loud wolf whistle. Andrea jabbed his arm as Laura climbed into the back seat of the sleek white Cadillac. Her blonde hair, usually pulled up into a ponytail, fell loosely over her shoulders. She wore more makeup than usual, and her cream-coloured pantsuit hugged her body in ways that drew attention. Cal complimented her, telling her she looked fabulous. He was used to seeing plain-Jane Laura at his house in sweatpants, baggy shirts, and no makeup. His friend Jonathan would be impressed. Not only did Laura look stunning, but the vibrant woman she had grown into made her fun to be around. Her kindness also drew people to her.

Jonathan had lost his wife three years earlier after a year-long battle with brain cancer. Unable to have children, he and his wife poured themselves into their careers. Their life was busy with his position as regional manager of a top Canadian bank and Brenda working as a district sales manager for a franchised women's clothing store. Since her passing, Jonathan felt lonely but grateful to have friends who included him at dinner parties and social events. Despite the time spent at work, he was happy to socialize at the golf course or watch sports with friends.

As a single mom with a young son, Tyler was Laura's first priority, and whoever was interested in her had to be interested in her son as well.

Meeting at a local restaurant was an easy way to be introduced to someone new. If they didn't connect, Laura could go home the same way she had arrived at the restaurant, with her friends. But she liked Jonathan the moment she met him. He was a handsome man, over six feet tall, prematurely gray, and athletic looking. He appeared a little shy but very down to earth. She loved his casually sophisticated style. He wore Calvin Klein navy coloured dress jeans and a white Pierre Cardin golf shirt. The shirt showed off his tan, which she assumed he had from golfing.

Dinner was enjoyable with lots of laughter. The men had been friends for many years and liked telling stories about each other. Laura and Andrea joined in with stories of their own. It was a warm and comfortable atmosphere that allowed Laura and Jonathan to have their own conversation as well. As dessert was served, he quietly asked her if he could drive her home. Laura had not felt an attraction like this to a man for many years. She felt comfortable in his presence, and on the drive home when he asked to see her again, she agreed. It wasn't too long before their dating became a regular occurrence and, twelve months after their first date, they were married.

Jonathan immediately adopted Tyler who became the son he had always wanted. The two were inseparable and one would never know that Jonathan had not fathered Tyler. He was a devoted father and the love between them grew every day. Laura had told Jonathan about Tyler's biological father, their brief affair, and the child support he had provided until his sudden death. They agreed that at some point in time they would share the information with Tyler. But the years passed quickly, and the happy family of three became a happy family of five.

Janessa was born when Tyler was eight, and Susie followed when he was nine. The Winters household was busy, happy, and blessed—a typical suburban family. There had been challenges through the years but, on the whole, life was very good to them.

CATHIE

With David Jr. off to Saskatoon, it wasn't long before Cathie realized how much she missed him. Anna and Olivia were beautiful girls, but she missed her son. He had always made time for her and shared all that was going on in his life. She never worried about who he was with and what he was doing. He was a smart, sensible young man.

David Jr. continued to be a model young adult into his later teenage years, and Cathie was thankful. Since he had moved to Saskatoon, things changed at home. Anna was going through a phase Cathie hoped would pass quickly. Her recent mood swings and lack of respect grew daily, and Cathie began to see a major change in her daughter. Sweet sixteen was turning into scary sixteen, and Cathie felt not only frustrated but concerned about Anna's erratic behaviour. Late nights on the phone, messy bedroom, and constant arguing. She certainly knew what teenage girls were like, having heard from her friends and coworkers—hormonal changes and boyfriends, for starters. But this seemed different. Anna's friends no longer came to the house, and her best friend, Callie, hadn't been there for weeks.

When Cathie brought up Callie's name, Anna shrugged it off.

"We aren't friends anymore," she said.

This concerned Cathie and, on one afternoon, she decided to contact Callie.

"Mrs. Bryant! So good to hear from you. How are you doing?"

Following a few minutes of small talk, Cathie asked what was going on between her and Anna.

Callie shrugged. "Anna has new friends at school. A tougher crowd, and not one I care to associate with. I'm concentrating on getting through my classes, and I guess that's not exciting enough for Anna. Mrs. Bryant, I'm really worried about her. She's changing. I know she's really missing David, but I'm still worried."

Callie's words confirmed what Cathie had been thinking: Something strange was going on with her daughter. They agreed to stay in touch and keep each other informed.

Cathie planned to chat with Anna later that evening. When she returned home from work, only Olivia was home. She was in tears and very distraught when Cathie walked into the kitchen.

"What's wrong?" she asked.

"I don't know where Anna is!" Olivia said in a broken voice. "She called me a few minutes ago and said she wasn't coming home. She told me to go into her bedroom and take all the money from her jewelry box and put it in a Ziplock bag and put it on the front doorstep at six o'clock. She just called ten minutes ago. Mom, what's going on? I don't know what to do!"

Olivia's tears continued to flow, and Cathie tried to console her daughter.

"What money?" she asked as calmly as she could. "Where was Anna calling from? Did she say where she was?"

Olivia reached into her sweater pocket and handed a large wad of money to her mother. Cathie gasped when she saw the stack of hundred-dollar bills.

Oh my God! What's going on! She grabbed her phone and called Anna's number. A gruff male voice answered.

"What do you want?"

"I want to speak with Anna!"

"She's not here."

"I want to speak with my daughter!"

"I told you. She's not here. But I hear you have my money at your house. We'll be there at six to get it, so if you want to see your daughter alive, you'd better have it ready and sitting on your front step. Remember, six o'clock."

The phone went silent.

Cathie was frantic. This could not be happening. She called 911. What should she do? Where could she go? She did not want to put either of her daughters in danger. The 911 operator answered right away. Cathie described what had happened, and the operator advised her to immediately leave the house with the money and come to the police station.

"Bring your cell phone, Mrs. Bryant, so we can trace the call."

Distraught and trembling, Cathie gestured to Olivia to take the money then pushed her toward the car. She silently prayed she was doing the right thing. How could this be happening?

When they arrived at the police station, they were whisked into a private room with two special officers. Between sobs and tears, Olivia explained the call she had received from Anna. Cathie then filled in her part of the story, informing them about her daughter's strange behaviour in recent months. Their conversation was documented and recorded as she spoke. The police wasted no time in dispatching officers to Cathie's home in unmarked cars. This was the break they were waiting for. A new drug ring had come into Calgary six months before. They knew the leader of the ring was Gustavo Gonzales from Mexico. He had come to Canada a few years previously and worked under the disguise of a school janitor for the past eighteen months. The police had been watching the school as the drug activity increased. There were several key players, of which Anna Bryant was one, but she was unaware she was being used and now framed by the drug ring.

Initially, Anna was selected by this gang through one of her teachers, Eduardo Menzies. Eduardo had been a teacher at Riverside Meadows High School for the past five years. A well-liked man originally from Mexico City, he had been involved with the Mexican cartel years earlier. When he arrived in Canada, the laws were not as strict as they currently are, and he was able to get into the country fairly easily. He had changed since leaving Mexico and lived a decent life until, in recent months, he and Gustavo Gonzales became friends. Unbeknownst to Eduardo, the friendship was a ploy to move the drug lords into the school.

Cathie felt gobsmacked by all she was hearing. Her life since David's passing had become quiet and ordinary. What unravelled before her now was like watching a movie. How would it all end? Would Anna get away safely? Was Anna doing drugs or was she just a runner for the Mexican cartel?

"Mrs. Bryant—"

She heard the officer say her name and was jarred back to reality.

"—This is what we need you to do. We'll set up recording devices so we can track Anna's phone when you call her. We know Anna won't be permitted to answer, so you must *demand* to speak to her. We have to delay the time of their picking up the money, so tell them you won't be able to have it on the step until seven o'clock tonight."

Time was running out—it was already five-thirty. They had just over an hour and a half to accomplish their plan. Anna would be brought home and dropped off, and Cathie would be in the house.

ANNA

How did she get into this mess? All she wanted was to be loved and accepted. At sixteen, she had started to explore and experience life. She was a model teenager. No issues at home, no challenges for her mother. She was an average student who played by the rules and kept her nose clean, at least until a few months ago. Anna and Callie had been inseparable since kindergarten. When they weren't at each other's homes, they were on the phone chatting. They spent so much time together that when Cathie did laundry, she often washed both Callie's and Anna's clothes. Cathie never had much to worry about. When David Jr. was around, so were the girls. She secretly had thought Callie had a crush on David, and once he had moved to Saskatoon, there wasn't much reason to be at the Bryant household. Especially now that Anna had changed her friends.

With Anna feeling David's absence, she sought male companionship elsewhere. She found most of the boys at school boring, and she had known them most of her life. Now she sought someone new. Austen Kelly had been introduced as the "new guy" in school a few weeks after first semester had begun, and her interest was piqued. His body piercings, tattoos, and brush cut made him stand out, and she liked that. She had been raised to not judge people by looks, so she gave him the benefit of the doubt and took time to get to know him.

As the new guy at school, he easily attracted attention. She paid attention to him in class and who he made friends with. After a couple of weeks, Anna knew he was different. He had an edge to him she had never seen in anyone else his age. His attitude toward the teachers, and lack of respect for people, made him look cool in her eyes.

Before long, they were an item, and she was in love. She was smitten with his bad-boy ways, but it bothered her that he showed no interest in going to her home or meeting her family. With the exception of a few male friends, he spent all his time with Anna. He always seemed to have a lot of cash on hand. Maybe that was why he wasn't interested in getting to know her friends. He even insisted she end her friendship with Callie.

During the past couple of days, she began to feel uncomfortable with Austen. She hadn't told her mother about him, and now she knew why. Red flags popped up everywhere, and she had been too blind to see them.

Austen and his friend, Gustavo, were holding her hostage in the school, now empty of teachers and students. Recent incidents in other schools had caused the school board to pass a ruling that schools close by four p.m. The only people permitted on school premises were the janitors. Anna had met Austen after school that day at their favourite coffee shop. Things had been fine until he received a phone call that he instantly answered. After a nervous conversation, he told her he had forgotten something at school and that they needed to go back. His short temper caused Anna some concern.

The school, by policy, was locked when they arrived. Increased gang activity had forced safety measures to be put in place. Gustavo Gonzales met them at the door, which Anna thought was unusual, as if it had been prearranged. Gustavo led them to the Janitor Room, and Anna asked why they needed to be there.

"Shut up and sit in the chair," Austen said.

Unsure of what was happening, Anna began to cry, which further irritated Austen.

"I told you to sit there and shut up!"

He grabbed her and shoved her toward the chair, tying a scarf around her mouth to silence her, then binding her hands and feet. Fear overpowered Anna. Her palms were sweaty, and she felt nauseated. Austen's phone rang again, and all she could hear was his side of the conversation.

"Yes, she has the money. I gave it to her earlier this week. Yes, I'll have her call her sister and make sure the money is on her front doorstep. No! The police don't know anything. I'm not stupid, Lono!" he exclaimed in exasperation. "We've done all this before. Quit yelling at me! I know what I'm doing."

Anna now saw the trouble she was in. What she thought was a romance was a cash deal.

Gustavo left the Janitor Room and when he returned, Eduardo Menzies was with him. When Eduardo saw Anna tied and gagged, he too now was involved in something more than a friendship with a fellow Mexican. Eduardo had connected Anna and Austen thinking it would be a good way to help Austen as a newcomer. From previous run-ins with the law in Mexico, Eduardo knew not to cause any problems. He played along with Austen and Gustavo as if he knew exactly what was happening. He didn't want to cause any harm to himself or Anna. Austen told them that they had work to do. Anna had money at her house for Lono Rodriguez, a friend of Austen's. They had called Anna's sister, telling her to put the money on the front step by six o'clock that evening. Eduardo would drive them to Anna's house, Austen would grab the money, and Gustavo would be on the lookout for neighbours or suspicious people lurking around. Anna and Eduardo were to stay in the car. When Austen got the money, the four of them would head south to the USA.

As Anna listened, more tears fell. How did she get involved with these people? What would happen to her mother and sister? She didn't have time to think. Austen pulled the scarf away from her mouth and held the phone to her ear as he called her sister. She relayed the message to Olivia. They would be there by six to pick up the cash.

EDUARDO MENZIES

Moving to Canada from Mexico City was not easy. Eduardo spoke little English, and most Canadians spoke little Spanish. Secondly, he had a troubled past. As the eldest of three children, he had been raised in a Catholic home by a single mother who worked hard to provide for him and two younger siblings. His father had left the family when Eduardo was only six. Bonita and Jorge were four and two, respectively. Eduardo barely remembered his father, but his love and dedication to his mother and his siblings was the true Catholic way in Mexico. They attended Catholic school, weekly mass, prayed the rosary, and shared what they had with those in need. This was the norm for Eduardo and his family until he had become entangled with the wrong crowd.

At fourteen, he started smuggling drugs out of Mexico and, at seventeen, he ended up in jail. Those were difficult years for Eduardo and his family, but a mother's prayers never go astray and, by the age of twenty-five, Eduardo was released. Being incarcerated had served him well, and his nine years served changed him. His faith in God grew, and he found a caring mentor who encouraged him to use his God-given talents. Eduardo was a competent student and used his time in jail to earn a teaching degree. God had a plan for him, and when he was offered the opportunity to come to Canada through a church in Calgary, he jumped at the chance. He was now making a positive difference in the world, helping teens with their life struggles. He was highly respected by his students, and his teaching career enabled him to send money to his family in Mexico. His life in Canada was quiet but fulfilling, and he was thankful for the abundant blessings God had given him.

Today, his past drug deals in Mexico were rapidly coming back to haunt him. The scene was too familiar. Anna was the hostage holding the drug money for Austen, the Canadian drug runner, and Gustavo, the next one up on the drug chain. Lono Rodriguez was the drug lord in Canada and leader of Satan's Rebellion, a well-known gang that had moved into Canada five years earlier. Initially, they were a lowkey gang; now, they were successfully growing their members and adding more criminal activity to larger cities. Eduardo mentally put the pieces of the puzzle together. Gustavo befriended Eduardo to use him as the driver in the getaway car. Eduardo needed to keep his mind clear and go along for the ride. He would do whatever it took to protect Anna and ensure her safety and the safety of her family.

Watching her fight back tears, Eduardo had to find a way to assure her he was on her side and would protect her.

CATHIE

The police were in position at Cathie's house. The SWAT team was in place and wore full body armour complete with helmets, leg pads, bulletproof vests, and face shields. Guns were in place, as were the officers who would take down the getaway car.

Olivia remained at the police station where she would be safe. She was highly emotional and shook with fear when her mother prepared to leave. Before she left the police station, Cathie called Anna's phone and made a deal with Gustavo Gonzales. The money would be left on the front step at seven p.m. that night in return for the safety of her daughter. She would be at the house alone. Gustavo had been blunt.

"Okay, I'll meet you at seven, but if you bring the cops, Anna will die!"

Cathie felt uneasy. She was at the house but not alone. A female police officer accompanied her. Constable Silver was dressed in Cathie's clothing and wearing a wig that matched her hair. Driving by or looking from a distance, no one would suspect she wasn't Cathie. Several police officers were camouflaged in the caragana bushes in front of the house. Four snipers were on each side of the house and two more behind the turrets on the rooftop. Cathie was astounded at how quickly this had come together. Something told her the police knew more than they were telling her.

The stage was set. It was six fifty-five p.m. Cathie's anxiety grew. What if they didn't release Anna? What if something went wrong? She silently prayed. *Please God, protect my Anna and bring her home safely.* At precisely seven o'clock, she heard the sound of a car driving down Elm Street. The police talked on their radios, and Officer Silver was ready to step outside with the money. The black 2012 Ford Fusion had two people in it. A second vehicle followed, remaining at a distance. The getaway car, black as well—a Ford Escape. Cathie could see Anna in the passenger seat.

Officer Silver opened the front door and placed the Ziplock bag with the fake bills on the doorstep. Two men wearing dark clothes and balaclavas jumped out of the car and, while one ran to the front step to get the money, the second one scanned the neighbourhood with a powerful rifle. Austen had the money in his hands, and the getaway car raced down the street with the two thieves ready to jump in.

The driver swerved past the two thieves and sped away. Cathie's heart stopped. No Anna. A commotion erupted followed by hollering, sounds of gunshots, more hollering. Police officers everywhere. Two men on the ground in handcuffs. Cathie heard Officer Silver shouting.

"It's over! We got them!"

Cathie was hysterical and in tears. Where did the getaway car go? Why didn't they pick up the thieves? Where was Anna? The police were so focused on the two men in the black Ford Fusion they missed seeing that Anna was gone in the getaway car with a third accomplice. The two apprehended men had been shot but not fatally. The police needed them alive. There was a gang in Mexico associated with these two and, at long last, the police would be able to put a dent in the criminal activity coming into Canada from Mexico.

Once the police took the two fugitives away, the black Ford Escape pulled up in front of the house. Anna jumped out and ran, sobbing, to her mother. They fiercely clung to each other. Eduardo Menzies, driver of the getaway car, stood behind Anna.

"Great job, Mr. Menzies!" Officer Silver said. "You were amazing! Let's go inside. We need to get a statement from each of you so we can put this to rest."

They went inside where Cathie and Anna heard the whole story.

Gustavo Gonzales was one of Mexican drug lords. He had arrived in Canada with the sole purpose of transporting drugs from Mexico. What better place to set up than through work at a school? He had a perfect, fake resumé, enabling him to enter the school system. Nine months earlier, he had befriended Eduardo Menzies whose previous corrupt lifestyle had enabled him to easily catch on to Gustavo's intentions. Eduardo reported him to the RCMP then became an undercover civilian for them. In his role as a teacher, he watched the drug setup unfold, playing along with Gustavo's plan and knowing Austen Kelly was the next target. He had figured out from the beginning that Austen was a drug runner and kept the RCMP informed. When Anna became involved with Austen, Eduardo knew then that things were heating up. His drug dealings in Mexico had followed the same script.

Drug lords set up in a new area and welcomed teens who had previous dealings with drugs. They were enticed by the promise of big money. Eduardo kept the police informed about everything happening at the school. When Gustavo made plans to collect the money from Anna's home, Eduardo knew he would be able to keep her safe once he had her in the getaway car. When Cathie and Anna heard the whole story, they were speechless. This explained how so many innocent teens were mixed up with the worst people. Anna was safe, and the one hundred thousand dollars in drug money was handed over to the police. Olivia would be home shortly, and Eduardo Menzies was now a hero and new friend.

In the days that followed, the police stayed closely connected to Anna and Eduardo, and counsellors were readily available to assist the family in dealing with the trauma they had experienced. This could have turned out so much worse. When Cathie went to bed that night, she thanked God for his blessings and protection. She would call David Jr. in the morning to tell him the news. It had been quite a day!

DAVID JR.

The first few months of university were a challenge and distinctly different from high school. There was a lot of adjusting and settling in, but David Jr. loved it. His roommates were amiable, and he met new friends. The university had an excellent basketball team, and he and his teammates became a close group. With weekly basketball practices, games, friends, and school, his life was hectic. He was able to keep things going well—with the exception of getting home more often. He had missed Thanksgiving, which devastated his mother, but he did get home for a couple of weeks at Christmas, and that kept everyone happy.

With the new year upon him, and another hectic semester ahead, he knew he wouldn't get home again until Easter. Love of basketball outweighed much of university life. His roommates loved to party, and while he spent time with his friends, partying was not his passion. But his friends were considerate of his crazy schedule and partied elsewhere other than in the house they shared.

Toward the end of the second semester, David was invited to a windup basketball party. It was always fun getting together with current friends and meeting new ones. The cheerleaders of the basketball team joined the party, and that night was when he first laid eyes on Janessa. She was a pretty blonde girl, short in stature but big in personality. Her kind brown eyes captured his heart as soon as she spoke. He had grabbed a beer from the bar when she came up and introduced herself. He had seen her at the games, but her beauty and warm smile somehow had escaped him then. He had dated other girls before, but Janessa was different. They spent the evening chatting and getting to know each other. She was from Saskatoon, and this was her first year on the cheerleading team. She asked him lots of question about himself. Where was he from? What was his major? The evening passed quickly, and they exchanged phone numbers before leaving the party.

The cheerleaders had made a pact at the beginning of the year, agreeing they would leave parties with the same friends they had arrived with. This was a protection pact on campus, a way the girls took care of each other. It also ensured that if someone had too much to drink, their friends would take care of them. With date-rape drugs on the incline in larger cities, girls now travelled in groups.

A week passed before David gave Janessa a call. He had been busy tying up loose ends before the semester ended. His plan was to return to Calgary for the summer, and he knew his mother was counting on seeing him. However, he had been offered a summer-student position at the university in the Human Resources Department. The pay was substantial, and it was in his best interest to take the job, as it would look good on his résumé. The university rarely offered these positions to first-year students, but it did add to his already frenzied week.

Janessa had hoped to hear from him, and when a week passed with no phone call or text, she wrote him off like all the others. Too bad! He had seemed so nice, and she felt there was a connection on his part. Her cheerleader friends liked him as well. Maybe it just wasn't meant to be.

When David called her on Saturday afternoon, she was taken by surprise. He apologized for not calling sooner as promised and told her about his crazy week.

"I'd love to take you out for coffee tomorrow if you don't have any plans."

She was thrilled. They made a date to meet for coffee at Starbucks the next afternoon on campus. An official date! Each was as excited as the other.

LAURA

After the excitement of the drug bust, Mr. Menzies became a frequent visitor at the Bryant home. There was much to share about the incident and much healing needed. Eduardo and Anna had been through a frightening time, but now they were celebrities. The bust hit national news, and reporters wanted a piece of the action.

Laura stayed up late one night and saw the news flash. Major drug bust in Calgary. Girl kidnapped! Two felons arrested. Sixteen-year-old Anna Bryant and her teacher, Eduardo Menzies, both safe and did not sustain any injuries. When she heard the name Anna Bryant, the wheels began to turn. She had not heard the Bryant name for a long time, and her mind flashed back to the passing of David Bryant twelve years earlier. Tyler's father. The affair from so long ago. What were the chances that this could be Tyler's half-sister? She shook her head and turned off the television.

Don't go down that path. No need to open a door that was closed so long ago.

But when a door is meant to be opened, the message keeps showing up. Anna Bryant and Eduardo Menzies. Their names were in *The Globe and Mail*, *The Calgary Herald*, *The Saskatoon Star Phoenix*, and many other Canadian papers. Nightly for weeks, their pictures were splashed across television screens. A drug bust this size had shut down a huge drug ring and prevented substantial amounts of drugs from entering Canada. Austin Kelly, the Canadian drug runner, Gustavo Gonzales, the Mexican drug lord, and Lono Rodriguez, the gang leader, had all been arrested. All three would be extradited to Mexico. The sixteen-year-old female student and the Canadian school teacher were Canada's newest celebrities.

Every night when Laura saw Anna Bryant, she became more convinced she was the daughter of David Bryant. Nothing of Anna's background was ever mentioned and, gradually, when the drug news died down, Laura let the story die as well. She never shared any of it with her family, and David Bryant's memory was buried once again.

CATHIE

People across Canada talked about the drug bust, and the school buzzed with excitement. How could a raid of this magnitude take place at a local school with so few people aware of it?

Anna was ecstatic. She loved the notoriety, but her mother was concerned. Her fear was that Anna would suffer nightmares, but the excitement seemed to overshadow the expected post-traumatic stress. Eduardo's visits to their house became more regular and, though Cathie really liked him, signs of a romance brewing between Eduardo and Anna left her uncomfortable. There was a substantial age difference between the two, Anna being only sixteen. Student-teacher relationships at school were unacceptable, and it might be time to have a chat with both of them. For Anna, it was more likely a high-school crush. For Eduardo, who knew? All she knew was that this was heading down a path she would prefer to avoid.

Cathie had trouble sleeping at night, reliving the episode, but Olivia seemed none the worse for the ordeal. Cathy missed having David Jr. around, especially at times when she needed someone to talk with. She shared the details with him and what was currently going on at home.

David Jr. had seen it all on the news and was shocked to learn his high school was involved. Cathie wished he lived closer but was happy he had settled in well and enjoying life in Saskatoon. The opportunity he had been given to work as a summer student at the University of Saskatchewan was a once-in-a-lifetime chance, and she was so proud of him. With the change of plans for David Jr., Cathie and the girls would definitely travel to Saskatoon in the coming weeks. It would do them all good to have a change of scenery.

She mentioned her lack of sleep, and David Jr. suggested she see a professional to discuss her concerns. Her mind continually relived the events of the raid and Anna's involvement. He also reminded her there were counsellors who could help her work through difficult situations. He was concerned and still felt like he was the man of the house though six hours away. Cathie reassured him she would look into counselling.

The weeks went on, and her sleep continued to be interrupted by nightmares and worry regarding Eduardo and Anna. She finally reached a breaking point and decided it was time to seek help. She contacted her employee-assistance program and was grateful to speak with a man who, after hearing her story, said she was dealing with post-traumatic stress disorder (PTSD). An appointment was booked for the following day with a counsellor familiar with the condition. Cathie's relief was palpable after the first two-hour session. Future appointments were booked, and the counsellor felt confident a few more sessions would get her back to feeling more in control.

EDUARDO MENZIES

One night, when Eduardo came by for dinner, Cathie thought it was time to approach the subject of his and Anna's relationship. Anna and Callie had plans to study at the library, and Olivia was at a friend's house. She didn't want to hurt his feelings, and she broached the subject cautiously while he helped her clear the dishes.

"Eduardo, I know you love to be fed, and we enjoy having you here. But why do you like coming to our place so often?"

Cathy was honest and told him he was always welcome then asked him outright if he had an interest in Anna. He blushed a little before admitting he was more interested in Anna's mother than in Anna. The Bryants had become his family over the past few months, and he had come to love Anna and Olivia like younger sisters, wanting to protect them.

Cathie suddenly felt ridiculous and didn't know what to say. She certainly didn't see this coming. Eduardo was fifteen years younger than she was, and she certainly had no interest in him. She had been so absorbed by what she thought was a relationship between Eduardo and Anna that she never noticed the longing in his eyes when he looked at her. She immediately set the record straight.

"Eduardo, you are like a son to me and are always welcome in our home. I appreciate you being here for me and the girls, but you need to find someone closer to your own age."

He was not surprised by her comments and felt thankful she was honest with him and happy he remained welcome. At least he still had a family here he could stay connected to.

CATHIE

Seasons passed and David Jr. was now in his third year of university, living full time in Saskatoon. He continued to achieve excellent grades, but his trips back to Calgary were less frequent. In a recent conversation with his mother, he mentioned dating a new girl named Janessa. Nothing too serious, though, as their schedules did not allow much time together. Cathie and her girls went to visit a couple of times, and the girls loved being with him. He showed them around Saskatoon and introduced them to his male friends, which the girls loved as it made them feel special.

Anna was giving serious thought to attending university, and she often questioned him about living in Saskatoon and what he loved about university life. She had graduated from high school the previous year and was taking a year off to find herself and figure out what she wanted. She and

Eduardo stayed casual friends and, once Eduardo knew there was no future for him with Cathie, his visits became less frequent. He was now dating one of the teachers at the high school and appeared genuinely happy. Anna and Callie were back to being best friends and spent all their time together. Anna thought journalism might be an option to consider for next fall but was still undecided. She thought heading to a new city might give her the excitement she was looking for.

Life was like a boat on calm waters throughout the past few months, and it felt wonderful. Cathie recently had begun dating a new friend she had met online, and Olivia would graduate from high school the following year. The new relationship with Daniel was light and friendly. He was a man of faith with a quiet personality but lived his life with passion. He was handsome, tall, and treated Cathy and her girls with kindness.

When David Jr. met him, he felt happy for his mother. It was strange to see her with a man, but he saw how delighted she was having someone to share her life with. Daniel had been divorced for years and had no children. He worked for one of the big five chartered Canadian banks and held the position of senior vice-president. He and Cathy enjoyed movies, golf, and long walks, and their time together was often spent at her home. Life moved along nicely, and there was a level of peace that Cathie thoroughly enjoyed.

It is said, however, there is often a calm before the storm.

DAVID JR.

The relationship between David Jr. and Janessa had grown serious unbeknownst to his family.

It hadn't occurred to him that he didn't spend enough time with Janessa. His position at the university was very important to him and his employers were thrilled with how committed he was to his job. He had learned his strong work ethic from his mother and his employers seemed grateful he had been taught so well. It was hard to find committed employees these days.

Janessa never complained so he was sure everything was great between them which it was. Love will do that. He loved everything about her, but never found the words to express it. Instead, he tried to show her by how he treated her when they were together. He opened car doors, walked on the outside close to traffic, and always held her hand.

Yet, even after dating for two years, they still had not met each other's families. David knew that was about to change.

They had booked a trip together to Lake Diefenbaker for a special getaway. High stress at work with tight deadlines didn't allow them many weekends together. They were both ready for time away. David had dreamed of this weekend for a long time. With a bottle of champagne in the cooler and an exquisite sapphire and diamond ring tucked in his suitcase, his heart beat faster than usual.

Would she be surprised? Would she say yes? Janessa didn't know it, but David had fallen deeply in love with her and was ready to take the next step. He couldn't wait until dinner that night when he would ask her to marry him.

JANESSA

Janessa had fallen in love with David from the start. What was there to not love about him? He was kind, gentle, treated her with respect, and was fun to be around. He had never expressed deep feelings for Janessa, but she was content to see him whenever it worked out. She was aware he wasn't dedicated to calling her all the time, but they had no set agenda, and she was willing to wait for him no matter how long it took.

So, she put her life on hold waiting for him. Her schedule was full between work, school, and social events, but when David reached out to her, she made herself available.

Her friends were not as happy with the relationship. They said David was holding Janessa on a string, and yanking whenever it was convenient for him. But Janessa knew they were unaware of how hard he worked and what a committed employee he was.

But now they'd get a weekend away together. Janessa was thrilled. Her friends, less so.

"He's taking you on a joy ride."

"He's not committed to you."

She felt frustrated with them and had grabbed her coffee and overnight bag and headed outside without saying goodbye.

She waited outside for him because she was annoyed with her friends and their remarks about David not being "a good fit for her."

Her roommates watched from the apartment window and discussed David and Janessa's relationship.

"I hope she knows what she's doing," Heather said. "A weekend away with a guy you may decide is not for you won't be much fun." Unbeknownst to her friends, the window was slightly open and Janessa heard their comments.

She saw the girls looking out the window. Who cares what they thought? They weren't her parents. She had moved out of her parents' home and in with her girlfriends to experience life and, up to this point, she had done nothing wrong.

Things with David were slow and cautious; they hadn't even had sex yet. She knew what she wanted in a relationship and that she would not be a one-night stand. Too many of her friends had become pregnant in their later years of high school or their first year of college. Maybe she *was* a little old-fashioned in her thoughts, but she was comfortable with that.

Right now, she was excited about going away with David. Time to concentrate on each other and enjoy the downtime. He had been working so hard, and she knew he could use the much-needed break.

WEEKEND GETAWAY

David appeared on time at ten a.m. She smiled as his flashy red car turned into the parking lot. Her heart did somersaults. She so loved this man.

She wore her Lululemon pink shorts and T-shirt. Her hair was tied back in a high ponytail, and her trendy Ray-Ban sunglasses blocked out the bright morning sunlight.

She was excited and a little anxious. Unknown to her, David was anxious as well. He commented on how beautiful she looked, which surprised her. This was the first time he shared such sentiments with her. He was so handsome sitting behind the wheel of his car, his dark hair and eyes looking much darker against his white Tommy Hilfiger T-shirt.

Springing out of the car, he leaned in for a quick kiss, and set her overnight bag onto the back seat. He walked around to the passenger side and opened the door for her. As always, he treated her like a lady. The vehicle was packed, and they were ready to go. Two coffees and muffins were now on the console—he had thought of everything. The drive to the lake was glorious, the day hot and sunny with a slight breeze. They sped down the highway with the convertible top down, singing with the tunes on the radio, and holding hands. Their hearts were full.

The drive was only ninety minutes and, as they neared the park, the view took Janessa's breath away. It had been several years since Janessa had visited the park, and she was astounded by the beauty of the trees and water. Saskatchewan was sometimes described as a boring, flat prairie with no trees, but not here. Southwestern Saskatchewan was magnificent, with Lake Diefenbaker as a reservoir and bifurcation lake. Her eyes feasted on the trees and bushes and the way the sun glistened on the blue water.

David drove up to the row of quaint cabins and stopped at the main office. The friendly receptionist was knowledgeable and helpful, offering information and brochures about the lake and the amenities of the resort. When they checked into their room, they were pleasantly surprised by how charming it was. Nostalgic and homey from the patchwork quilt on the bed to the basket of fruit on the table. The resort had covered all amenities and then some.

They had no special plans for the afternoon, but David had arranged to go waterskiing the next day. Neither had waterskied before and both were excited to give it a try. There were boat-and-ski rentals, and a driver and spotter could be hired for a reasonable price. They were booked for ten a.m. the following day.

It didn't take long to unpack their things. They were anxious to wander around the resort and explore the lake area. The early part of the afternoon was spent investigating walking trails, gift shops, and stopping for ice cream at the local favourite place, The Big Moo. With numerous flavors of homemade ice cream, choosing wasn't easy, and Janessa finally decided on Orange Pineapple. David was happy to find his favourite, Cookies and Cream. They strolled, hand in hand, eating their ice cream, quietly conversing and happy to be with each other.

After a long walk on the lakeshore and a few games of Horseshoes and Bean-Bag Toss, they headed back to the cottage to get ready for dinner at the Star Quarter Restaurant.

Janessa made mental notes on everything. She wanted to remember all the details of the weekend to share with her roommates. She was sure by the time she got home they all would be friends again. As they walked from their cottage to the restaurant an hour or so later, the sun was slowly descending in the sky. Sunlight still reflected on the water, and the orange and white lilies surrounding the restaurant made her feel like they were in paradise.

When they arrived at the restaurant, the hostess seated them in a secluded booth overlooking the pier, offering yet another spectacular view. Boats were still cruising on the lake with lots of people waterskiing. There were several boats tied up further down the pier, and David and Janessa talked about how much fun the next day would be when they tried their skills at waterskiing.

A glass of wine before and during dinner left them feeling mellow and romantic.

"Oh, wow!" David said. "Look at how young that little girl is to be waterskiing!"

Janessa turned to look out the window, and David took the ring from his pocket. When Janessa turned back to respond, David was ready.

"Janessa, will you marry me? I've loved you from the first moment we met."

Their quiet, steady relationship had grown into deep love and respect for each other. Janessa's eyes filled with tears, and she replied with a resounding "Yes!"

David presented her with a sculptured solitaire diamond ring surrounded by sapphires. Its worth was part of the reason he had been working so diligently. He had wanted to ask Janessa to marry him months before. The overtime hours were challenging but it gave him the opportunity to buy the ring he knew she would love.

Janessa was beaming as David was placing the ring on her finger. The server came by to see if everything was satisfactory and whether they were ready for the dessert menu. When she saw Janessa's face, she knew something exciting had just happened. The newly engaged couple shared their news with her and, after she congratulated them, she made a grand announcement to everyone in the restaurant. Enthusiastic applause immediately followed, and many customers stopped by their table to congratulate them before leaving.

Wine continued to flow, making for a memorable evening. Janessa glowed, and David thought he had never seen her look so beautiful.

They would share the news with family and friends the next day after returning from their waterskiing adventure. Tonight was reserved for them and the intimacy they shared. It was a night they would never forget.

When David woke the next morning, Janessa lay beside him admiring her diamond ring.

"Good morning, beautiful!" he said, leaning over and kissing her cheek.

"Good morning, my love."

They had made love passionately the night before. It was everything she had dreamed it would be. She rolled over and placed her arms around his neck.

"I love you so much. I can't believe this is happening, and I'm so excited for our future together."

"Then let's get a move on!" David said. "We have a great day ahead of us, and when we conquer our fear of waterskiing, we'll come back and call our families."

JANESSA

The lake was perfect, and the skies were clear; it was another hot, sunny day. The reflection of the sun sparkled vividly on the water. Matthew, the boat driver and Ken, the spotter, were friendly and welcoming, and their instructions were easy to follow. David soon was up and standing on his skies. He took naturally to the sport, and watching him made Janessa's heart beat with pride.

Less athletic than David, she needed more time before cautiously raising herself onto her skis but felt confident once she stayed up.

"David, look at me!"

He cheered her on from the boat. "I knew you could do it, babe!"

She felt free as a bird, loved her new sport, and couldn't wait to call her parents and tell them the news of their engagement. More excitement still lay ahead with details of setting a date, finding a venue, choosing attendants, and shopping for a wedding gown and bridesmaid dresses.

They spent a few more hours on the lake taking turns skiing, falling, and being rescued by the driver who spun the boat around, picked them up, and allowed them to try again. Summer was Janessa's favourite time of year. Her heart sang with joy, the beauty of her surroundings, and the warmth of the sun.

When her legs couldn't handle more skiing, she waved to the spotter to let him know she was ready to come in. They still had twenty minutes of their booked time left, and David wanted one last ski lap.

This time he was too sure of himself. Showing off his moves, he let go of the rope with one hand, wildly waving with the other. His laugher could be heard across the lake and, briefly distracted, he lost control. One ski slipped from his foot and crossed over the other. He tumbled over and over with the skis going in every direction. Janessa screamed as disaster unfolded in front of her. David was underwater and in trouble.

Matthew swung the boat around, and Ken jumped into the water. Another boater saw what had happened and pulled up alongside them. Several people jumped into the water. Again, Janessa screamed incoherently at the sight of blood spreading outward from where she last saw David.

Time stood still before paramedics were on the frenzied scene. They took David's vital signs, stabilized his legs, then carefully placed him on a gurney. A large gash on his head and major internal bleeding had left him in critical condition.

Terrified, Janessa sat beside him in the ambulance that soon raced toward Saskatoon with sirens screeching. Urgency had prevented her from collecting personal belongings. Her phone as well as David's were in the locker room at the boat launch. She felt lost and confused. The love of her life lay unconscious on a stretcher in an ambulance. What started out as a romantic weekend had become a nightmare.

The paramedics hooked up David to oxygen and stabilized him. His being unconscious would prove beneficial in the long run. The driver radioed St. Paul's Hospital, giving the stats on their patient and their estimated time of arrival. As Janessa listened, she gulped back deep breaths and tears. The paramedic named Stephanie reached out and held Janessa's hand.

"We're doing everything we can to keep him comfortable."

Her colleague, Brett, kept a constant watch on David.

Stephanie tried to distract Janessa from her constant watch. She noticed the engagement ring on Janessa's left hand and commented on how beautiful it was. Janessa smiled and told her about the evening before—how David had surprised her.

"We were planning to tell our families later today."

David started to moan, and Stephanie and Brett turned their attention to their patient. Janessa was left alone with her thoughts.

When they arrived at the hospital, David was whisked off to surgery still unconscious. The nursing staff were very kind and took Janessa to a private room where she could call her family. One of the nurses brought her a cup of tea, introduced herself as Danielle, and asked her if she wanted anything. She motioned to the phone in the corner and told Janessa she could use it. For anything else, she could go to the nursing station. Danielle said she would be there for Janessa until her family arrived.

Janessa decided to contact David's family as soon as she had more news, but first, she called her mom.

"Mom, there's been an accident," she said, giving her mother a quick account.

"I'm at St. Paul's Hospital. Can you and Dad come right away?"

"Are you injured?" Laura asked.

"No, but David is badly hurt. Please hurry. I need you here, Mom. I'm scared." She began to shiver and looked down. "Oh, Mom? Can you bring me some clothes? I'm still in my bathing suit and cover up."

"We're on our way, honey. We'll be there as quickly as possible."

Her parents lived only twenty minutes away, and it would be a long twenty minutes until she could feel the arms of her parents around her. She thought about calling her roommates but decided to wait. It was more important to call David's family as soon as she had an update from the surgeon. Sitting alone in the private room, she curled up and sobbed. Their perfect weekend had turned tragic. David, her love, was in a coma and possibly on life support. In her anguish, she called out to the God of her childhood. *Where are you? I feel so alone!* She heard nothing but felt a little more at peace, as if she were not really alone.

She stepped outside of the room and was relieved to see her parents walking briskly down the hallway. She didn't need to be so strong on her own anymore, and she gave way to uncontrolled tears and emotions. Now she could share in full the trauma of what happened. Her mother handed her a Kleenex and saw the sparkling diamond ring. She was startled but said nothing. She knew Janessa had been seeing someone on and off but was unaware the relationship was serious. Janessa had mentioned David's name on occasion but had never introduced him. Now was not the time to ask questions about an engagement and an upcoming wedding. They both needed to be there to support their daughter through this difficult time. When Janessa's father went to get coffee and sandwiches, she and her mother sat and waited. Janessa was grateful for not having been quizzed about David and the ring. All she wanted was to hear he was going to be all right.

Her father walked into the room with steaming coffee and sandwiches followed by the surgeon who introduced himself as Dr. Friesen, the attending physician. He was a tall, thin man with a freshly shaven face and salt-and-pepper hair and looked to be in his late forties. He had a calm, quiet demeanor as he glanced at both women and then asked which was Janessa.

"I am, and these are my parents," Janessa replied.

Dr. Friesen nodded and first said how sorry he was then proceeded to tell them about David's condition.

"David has a severe gash on the back of his head. The cut was quite deep and required stitches. We know that the outer wound will heal in time, but we want to keep him in a medically induced coma for a few days. There is also internal bleeding in his stomach area and, right now, we're not sure where the bleeding is coming from. We're concerned about this."

Janessa tearfully leaned into her mother's arms for support.

"May I see him?" she asked.

Dr. Friesen gave his permission and escorted Janessa and her mother to the recovery room. David was hooked up to several machines: oxygen, IV for pain medication, and a catheter. His head was bandaged and there were several bandages on his abdomen. Janessa fell into her mom's arms sobbing. The only other sounds came from the beeping machines keeping David alive.

"I know how difficult this is for you," Dr. Friesen said to Janessa. "All we can do now is keep David comfortable and wait. I recommend that you and your family go home and get some rest and return in the morning. I hope by then there will be better news. Should anything change, the nursing staff will call you. But for now, we'll keep him sedated to give his body a chance to recover.

As they left the hospital, Janessa's parents suggested she spend the night with them. She was emotionally and physically exhausted, and the day had taken a heavy toll.

She was glad she had put on her bathing suit coverup after skiing. Still, it felt strange to be in a hospital wearing a bathing suit and coverup. Fortunately, she and her mother were the same size and she was grateful she was able to change once her parents arrived with extra clothing. If they got to the lake tomorrow, she would pick up David's vehicle and their belongings.

Resting in the back seat of her father's car, Janessa silently prayed that God would be with David and keep him comfortable through the night. Tomorrow would be a better day.

Their mood during the drive from the hospital to her parents' house was solemn. The massive green oak trees in full bloom and the lush green grass by the riverbanks always had made Janessa feel happy. But today, her mind was in turmoil as she thought about the day's events. When they reached her parents' house, her mother made them something to eat. She didn't feel hungry, but her mother encouraged her to have a few bites. When she tasted her favourite sweet and sour spaghetti and Caesar salad, she didn't realize how hungry she had been. Breakfast had been many hours ago, and she hadn't eaten at the hospital when her father arrived with sandwiches and coffee. With food and drink, she felt a little better. No questions were asked about her ring, and general conversation was minimal. There wasn't much to say. Janessa was exhausted and went to bed as the sun was setting.

Her night was restless with dreams of David and the accident. She woke several times and, as she lay in bed, she repeated prayers for his protection and healing. The hardest part was trusting God to take care of things.

She was up at seven a.m. and felt better after a long, hot shower and a change of clothes. Besides wearing the same size clothes, Janessa and her mother shared similar tastes in clothing. Her mother's clothes would work until they got to the lake and picked up her own things. She liked to look perfectly put together, but today none of that mattered. All she wanted was to get to the hospital and see David. Her mother had been up earlier and had coffee and breakfast ready. She knew Janessa would appreciate it, and when she came into the kitchen, her mother hugged her then served her a cup of coffee and a croissant with homemade raspberry jam. It was comforting to be home with her parents.

As Janessa finished eating, her father came into the kitchen. He hugged his girl and asked about going to Lake Diefenbaker to pick up David's vehicle and their belongings. Janessa called the hospital while her mother put the dishes away. There had been no change with David. He had remained quiet through the night, and the charge nurse promised she would call if there were any changes. Janessa left her parents' cell numbers with the ICU nurse until she was able to retrieve her own phone. They would stop at the hospital when they got back to the city.

She expected to call David's mother after speaking with the doctor. Since there had been no negative changes in David's condition, she agreed with her father that they drive to the lake right after breakfast. The ride today didn't compare to Friday, which seemed so long ago.

This time, the time passed quickly and, when they arrived at the cabin, though still distraught, Janessa smiled to herself, recalling the happy memories of Friday night. They had shattered so quickly.

Their cabin had been left in order, all their clothes put away, and the bed made before they had gone waterskiing. The room looked like no one had slept there, and it was easy to gather their belongings. Janessa grabbed the few toiletries from the bathroom, and they were set to go. Her father drove David's car back and Janessa and her mother followed in the family vehicle. The gratitude she felt for her parents was indescribable. She had taken them for granted for so many years. *How do people manage when they don't have family they can count on?*

They stopped by the reception desk to check out of the resort and let the manager know how David was doing. Janessa knew an incident report would need to be completed because of the accident location. As they chatted with the manager, he expressed his concern for David and Janessa.

"The staff were so excited about your engagement on Friday," he said. "When word got out about the skiing accident, our clients and staff were very concerned. Thank you for stopping by to give us an update. I'll be sure to let everyone know how David is doing. And please keep us informed. Tell him we're all praying for a speedy recovery!"

Janessa thanked him for his kindness. As they walked toward the car, her mother remarked on the kindness they had been shown but still said nothing about the engagement.

The trip back to the city was quiet with not much conversation. Janessa was preoccupied with how to tell David's family about the accident. She hoped the internal bleeding had stopped and that David would be able to make the call himself.

Laura was preoccupied with the engagement. She was so anxious to hear all the details.

The trip went by relatively fast and, after dropping David's vehicle at her parents' house, they headed back to the hospital. No change. David was still unconscious, but his colouring had improved significantly from the previous day. His head remained bandaged, and both of his eyes were now black from the blow to his head. Janessa sat with him and held his hand. Her parents stepped outside the room to give her privacy. They remembered the love they had felt for each other in the early days. It was fresh and euphoric. Now, their love was different, mature and deep. Their hearts broke for their daughter as they could feel her love for David and the pain she was going through.

After an hour, her father suggested they drive home.

Although she had reclaimed her belongings from the lake, Janessa stayed with her parents. She would need their love and support in the coming days, especially when she called David's family.

CATHIE

Cathie walked in the front door of her lovely home. She enjoyed going out for the afternoon but was happy to return to her sanctuary. The entrance was spacious and had been professionally decorated by a former coworker. Large windows on either side of the front door gave way to rays of sunshine peeking through the aster bushes in her yard. Sunlight made the hardwood floors gleam. She had spent a delightful afternoon with Daniel. Tennis followed by a barbeque and glass of Chardonnay at his house. She felt more comfortable with their relationship and sensed he felt the same way. Love was in the air.

"Alexa, play Michael Bublé!"

As the music played, she put her things away and smiled. Her heart was full. She had not felt this way in a very long time. The house was empty. Olivia and Anna were out with friends but would be home shortly. It was almost eight p.m., and school and work awaited them all tomorrow.

Her phone rang and she saw it was David Jr. calling. What a perfect way to end a weekend! She hadn't chatted with him since last Sunday.

"Hi!" she said light-heartedly. "Your timing is perfect. I just got in."

"Hello, Mrs. Bryant? Is this Cathie Bryant? David's mom?"

"Yes," she replied hesitantly.

"My name is Janessa. I'm David's girlfriend," the voice on the phone said.

Cathie immediately felt uncomfortable. "Where is David? Why are you calling me?"

"There's been an accident . . ."

Cathie's world started to crumble. "Oh my God! Is he okay? Where is he"?

Janessa took a deep breath and, as she calmly as she could, she relayed the events of the waterskiing accident.

Cathie had taken a seat on the couch. Déjà vu! Memories of her husband . . . the call from the hospital . . . the doctor telling her David was gone . . . the nausea in her stomach.

Janessa reassured her that David Jr. was resting comfortably but that he was in an induced coma for his own protection. She suggested Cathie call the hospital to get an update.

"I told the head nurse at the nursing station you would be calling."

Janessa gave her the number to the hospital.

Cathie felt a degree of relief now that she was thinking more clearly, but she was mentally making decisions. She would drive to Saskatoon in the morning to be with her son. It would be easier than taking a flight. She could get an early start tomorrow and would be in the city in less than six hours. She was grateful to Janessa for the call and told her so.

She then asked Janessa how she was doing. She was unsure of the seriousness of the relationship, but she could hear the stress in the girl's voice.

"I'm okay. I'm so grateful my mom and dad are here with me. Please let me know when you're coming. I look forward to meeting you. David speaks so highly of his amazing mom that I'm sure he'd want you here."

"I'll be in Saskatoon by tomorrow afternoon. I'll call you once I arrive."

After they exchanged goodbyes, Cathie called the hospital. When she had confirmation that David was stable, she started packing for her trip the next day. It may not be a bad idea for Anna and Olivia to join her. They would figure out the logistics once the girls got home.

LAURA

Laura was hurting for her daughter. They were having coffee before Janessa left for the hospital. The day was cloudy and cooler than normal, but the weather was supposed to clear by noon. Now was the time to ask a few questions about David. Obviously, they were engaged, but with the seriousness of David's injuries, thoughts of planning a wedding were not important right now. Laura got up from the table and returned with the coffee pot. Janessa held out her cup, and the diamond ring flashed in the morning light.

"That's a beautiful diamond ring you're wearing. Anything you want to share with your dad and me?"

They hadn't seen her for a week or more, and Laura didn't know when she had received the ring.

Janessa then told her parents about the weekend. Their blissful evening together, the fun supper, and the romantic proposal. How excited they had felt about waterskiing. Their plan to call both families to share the news when they returned to the cabin. As she cried, she confessed to her parents how scared she was. She had said yes to David's proposal.

"I'm not sure what the future holds, but I know I love him and, together, we'll get through this."

Laura and Jonathan got up from the table and hugged her.

"We're so excited about you and David, but first we need to get him back to good health," Laura said. "Hopefully, today, we'll have better news. Tell us a bit about this future son-in-law of ours," Laura said, smiling. "What's he like?"

"Mom, he's amazing. We met two years ago at a party, and I instantly fell for him. He's smart, kind, and so much fun to be with. Our relationship was casual for a long time, and that's why I never talked much about him or brought him home. I wasn't sure where it was all going. We both have busy lives, but in the last few months we've been seeing more of each other." She beamed with pride as she spoke of David. "I think I knew he was the one for me, but I wasn't sure he felt the same way. I was willing to wait and see where things went. He's the oldest in his family and has two younger sisters. His dad died when he was six years old, and his mom raised the three children while working full time for an insurance company in Calgary. He's very close to his mom and his sisters. They've come to see him a few times, but I haven't met them yet. I'm looking forward to meeting his mom, but I wish it was under better circumstances."

Laura felt better knowing more about David and the engagement. Janessa was not one to take things lightly and wouldn't rush into something unless she felt sure. She too looked forward to meeting David and his mother. The wedding and all it involved would be decided on at a later date. Her thoughts turned to Janessa and David. They had a lot to deal with at this point. *Let's take one day at a time.*

Did you reach David's family?" Laura asked.

"I did! His mom called me back this morning and she hopes to be at the hospital between two and three this afternoon."

Jonathan said he was glad she had moved back home temporarily until they found out more about David's injuries. Janessa agreed. She loved her roommates and had contacted them about the accident, but she knew she would be more comfortable with her parents. Luckily, she had the week off work, leaving her able to spend all her time at the hospital.

Laura said that David's mother was welcome to stay with them if she wished. She couldn't imagine how difficult it must be to be so far away and hear her child had been seriously injured. She felt blessed her children lived close by. Susie still lived at home, but Janessa and her brother, Tyler, had moved out after graduation. Having Janessa back home was just like old times. As they talked about David and his recovery, Laura said she would plan a few meals that week and extended the invitation for his mother to join them. She left the invitation in Janessa's hands, knowing how nervous she was about meeting Cathie. Maybe this would be the best way to see how well they connected.

When they finished breakfast and their conversation, Janessa got ready and left for the hospital. There had been no calls from the nurses, so that was a good sign.

CATHIE

The drive from Calgary to Saskatoon was a long one, and Cathie had decided to travel alone. Trying to arrange for the girls to have time off school and work would have been one more thing to deal with. All she wanted now was to see David Jr. She could always fly the girls to Saskatoon once he was in recovery. She had been able to reach her boss at home the night before and let her know of David Jr.'s accident. When she called Daniel to tell him, he wanted to travel to Saskatoon with her. He knew how close Cathie was to her son, but she was strong, and she felt it was better to go on her own this time. While waiting for the girls to come home, she had started packing and was upstairs in her room when she heard Anna and Olivia come into the house.

"Mom, are you home?" Olivia hollered.

"Up here!"

They raced up the stairs, laughing and shoving each other. It must have been a good afternoon. They got along well, reminding Cathie how grateful she was that they were good, easygoing girls.

Anna had a strange look on her face when she saw her mother packing, clothes strewn across the bed.

"What's up, Mom? Where are you going? Are you running away with Daniel?" Anna asked.

Cathie smiled. She wanted to gently tell the girls about David's accident and not put too much emphasis on his injuries until she knew more.

"There's been an accident. David's girlfriend, Janessa, called. He was injured while waterskiing, and I'm going to Saskatoon first thing in the morning."

Anna and Olivia ran to their mother and embraced her. They adored their big brother and hearing the news was devastating. Cathie tried to remain as calm as she could and reassured the girls David was doing well but didn't give them all the details. At this point, she didn't feel it was necessary.

While she packed her suitcase, the girls filled her in on their afternoon excursions with friends and hanging out at the local swimming pool. The weather was hot and sunny, and they had forgotten they were still in bathing suits and coverups. After assuring the girls David would be fine, Cathie finished her packing while the girls grabbed a bite to eat before showering.

She was on the road by seven a.m. with a thermos full of coffee and some muffins and apples to keep her going. She didn't want to stop too often. Her goal was to be in Saskatoon by early afternoon. It was unusually hot and sunny early in the morning, and she was grateful for air conditioning. She had witnessed a magnificent sunrise at five a.m. while having her coffee at home. Now, driving along the highway, she was struck by how beautiful the crops looked, peeking through the black soil.

Her mind returned to David Jr. She had called the hospital the night before to let the staff know she was coming to Saskatoon. The head nurse was kind and assured her David was holding his own and doing as well as could be expected. Cathie called again before she left the house and was advised there were no changes.

She tried again to distract her thoughts and was surprised by the beauty of the drive. She had never been to Saskatoon, though it was only six hours from Calgary. She loved downhill and cross-country skiing, but it was more the west country that attracted her, especially the majestic Rocky Mountains in all their splendour. Heading east of Calgary toward Saskatoon, the land was mostly flat and the road straight for miles. Mostly farmland with an oil derrick here and there. As a city girl, she knew little about farming. There were lots of John Deere green machines, and she wondered what they were for. Keeping her mind off what she would see when she got to the hospital was a helpful distraction. She had called Janessa before leaving home to let her know her approximate time of arrival would be between two and three p.m. They would meet at the hospital in David's room.

As she tried to focus on her driving, her mind wandered to questions about Janessa. What is she like? Is this relationship serious? David had mentioned Janessa's name a few times over the past year without disclosing much. The older David Jr. got, the more private he had become. Maybe not purposely but due to his busy life. She missed her son but understood he always had lots going on.

The trip went by faster than she had thought it would. A few stops for gas and bathroom breaks broke the monotony of continuous driving. The snacks she had packed helped keep her alert. Before too long, she saw the sign: *Welcome to Saskatoon*.

She had arrived!

JANESSA

The sun shone brightly in David's room and the reflection bounced off the machines, making tiny diamonds on the wall. Janessa held David's hand and spoke words of encouragement to him. She wasn't sure whether he could hear her, but the nurse on duty assured her there was no harm in talking to him.

"The doctor will be in later this afternoon to have a chat with you," she said. "We understand David's mom is coming from Calgary today, and I'm sure you'll appreciate having her here."

Janessa nodded in agreement. "We haven't met yet. I'm a little nervous but, yes, it will be good to have her here. Thank you for all that you're doing to keep David comfortable. The staff have been amazing."

The young nurse left the room as the heart monitor beeped quietly and the oxygen pump kept David's oxygen levels where they should be. Janessa so appreciated the kindness shown from all the hospital staff. They were caring and attentive not only to David's needs but made sure Janessa was all right too!

While she was deep in thought, she heard footsteps, and an unfamiliar woman walked into the room. Cathie stared in shock when she saw David. She looked at the young woman holding his hand.

"You must be Janessa," she said.

Janessa smiled shyly. "I am, and you must be David's mom."

They embraced then Cathie leaned down and hugged her son. She wasn't prepared to see him like this. The nurse walked in as she was pulling away from David with tears in her eyes.

"You must be David's mother."

With Cathie's acknowledgement, the nurse gave her details on her son's condition.

"He's resting well, and the doctor is pleased to see his head injury slowly healing. He took quite a blow from the skis, but we're still concerned about the internal bleeding. The doctor will discuss this with you when he comes by for rounds."

She excused herself and left Cathie and Janessa with David.

Cathie pulled a chair closer to the bed and, together, the women sat, each holding one of David's hands. They were both at the hospital for the same reason: they loved him. Cathie regained her composure after seeing him in a coma. It brought back memories of when she had seen her husband in a hospital bed. He looked like he was sleeping, but he had already passed from this world into the next. As difficult as it was to see her son hooked up to so many machines, she was grateful they were helping him breathe and keeping him alive. She had questions to ask Janessa. How did this happen? Where were they? How long had she and David been seeing each other? All her questions would be answered in the days ahead while she and Janessa kept vigil at David's bedside. For now, she would let the stories unfold as they may. She was glad Janessa was here with her son.

Two hours had passed when the doctor came in to see David. The nurse had been by a few times to check his vitals and change his IV. There was minimal change, and David continued to rest comfortably. Janessa and Cathie were quietly getting to know one another, and Janessa told her how they had met and how their courtship had evolved over the past two years.

She already had told her about the waterskiing accident, but no details of the proposal had been brought up. Janessa purposely left her engagement ring on the dresser at her parents' house. She wanted to get to know Cathie better and hoped she and David could share the news of their pending wedding when he woke up.

Dr. Friesen was a caring man and, though matter of fact about David's injuries, he was compassionate when speaking about him.

"David lost a lot of blood and has already received two transfusions. I'd like to wait another twenty-four hours before giving him a third. It also looks like one of his kidneys may have been damaged in the accident. We're still unsure of the extent of the damage, and I've scheduled an exploratory within the next couple of days. Right now, it's on a wait-and-see basis. Let's give him a couple more days. I'll have the nurses keep you informed. I know this is difficult, but the body has great capability to heal when we allow God to take control. Just trust and pray." And with that, he left the room to continue his rounds.

Cathie's fatigue set in. It had been a long day, and she needed sleep. She had been able to book a room at the Parktown Motor Inn right beside the hospital. It was booked for three nights, and she would soon see how long she may need to extend it.

Janessa decided to go home. It had been a long day for her as well. The beeping machines and the antiseptic smells made her feel nauseated. She admired how the nurses and doctors were able to be in an atmosphere of disease and death for long periods of time. She felt emotionally wrung out. Her parents had offered to come and sit with David for a while that evening, and she was going to take them up on their offer.

As they prepared to leave, Janessa and Cathie hugged and agreed to meet the following day or during the night if anything changed.

LAURA

Laura's husband was unable to join her at the hospital that evening so she went on her own. Janessa's siblings, Tyler and Susie, had been checking on her, and they would keep her company. She couldn't wait to share the excitement of her engagement to David. Everything had been put by the wayside after the accident, but she knew David would pull through and life could then move forward.

Laura sat in David's room a few hours later, quietly reading her book, when Cathie walked in. She had eaten and checked into her hotel room with the intention of lying down. She tried, but sleep would not come. Knowing her son was so close by, she wanted to spend as much time with him as possible.

"Oh, hi," Laura said. Both women were unsure of who the other was.

"Hi," Cathie replied. "I'm David's mom, Cathie."

"I'm Laura, Janessa's mom."

They greeted each other with a hug, and Cathie pulled up another chair close to the bed. The monitors beeped and hummed, and the women spoke quietly over them.

"I'm so sorry." Laura said. "I know how difficult this must be for you. You must be exhausted from your long drive today."

Cathie nodded in response to both points. "It has been a long day, but I want to be with David."

The mothers spent the next hour or so getting to know each other. They talked about their children and found that neither knew much about the relationship that had grown over the past two years.

Cathie was happy to have Laura with her, and the evening passed quickly. The night nurse came to check on David just before visiting hours were over. She said there was still no change but that was a good sign. He's in a deep sleep and that's what his body needed.

As they prepared to leave, the nurse promised Cathie she would call if anything changed. She also suggested that both women could return outside visiting hours if they wished.

"I've worked in ICU for many years, and I know how hard this is for you both."

Cathie's exhaustion set in. The long drive, her emotions at seeing her son in a coma, meeting Janessa and Laura for the first time. It was a lot to absorb in one day. As they walked out of the hospital, Laura invited her to join them for dinner the next day.

"As long as David is stable, I'd be happy to join you and your family," Cathie said. "Thank you so much for being there for him. I know he'll personally thank you when he wakes up."

They hugged each other again and said goodbye with promises to stay in contact.

When Laura got home, Janessa was waiting for her with a cup of tea.

"How is David?" she asked. "Is he still resting comfortably? I'm heading back to the hospital in the morning."

It had been a pleasant break to spend time with her siblings but, as David's future wife, her place was with him.

"Cathie returned to the hospital not long after I got there," Laura said. "She couldn't sleep. We had a good time chatting and getting to know each other."

As nothing was said about the engagement, Laura asked Janessa if she had told Cathie.

"No. As a matter of fact, I didn't even wear my ring today. But I will tomorrow and then I can tell Mrs. Bryant about our plans."

Laura looked up from the table. "Mrs. Who?"

"Mrs. Bryant, David's mom."

David's last name had never come up, and Laura hadn't heard that name in a very long time. David Bryant! What were the chances? Calgary had over a million people. Laura got up and went to the sink, not wanting Janessa to see the surprised expression on her face.

The back door opened, and Jonathan Winters entered the kitchen.

"Hello, ladies! How are my favourite gals doing tonight? And how's our patient?"

Janessa quickly filled him in on the events of the day. "There's been no change. He's still in the induced coma, but the nurse said that was good and his body will heal quicker. His mom, Cathie, arrived around three o'clock. She thought his sisters, Anna and Olivia, should wait and see how David is doing before coming to see him. She's staying at the Parktown Motor Inn, but Mom invited her for dinner tomorrow night. And I decided not to tell her about the engagement yet because she had so much to deal with already."

"Whoa!" said Jonathan, smiling. "That's a whole lot of information at one time. But I'm happy to hear David's mom is here, and I look forward to meeting her. I'm so glad too that David is still resting easily. I know how tough this is on you, kiddo," he said as he hugged her.

Laura busied herself with dishes at the sink, but her mind was racing. It felt like yesterday when she had picked up Tyler from daycare and was told her cheque had bounced. A flood of memories and emotions returned—like a movie playing in her mind. She could hear Janessa and Jonathan talking in the background without paying attention to what they were saying. She saw herself calling David to ask why his cheque had been returned. That was the day she found out he had died.

She remembered the feeling of loss as she read the obituary—not so much for David but for his wife and children. They had been a family she didn't know but to which she was connected. *Oh, my God, how could this be possible?*

"Mom, you okay?" Janessa asked. "You look like you're a million miles away."

Laura felt herself pulled back into the present.

Jonathan kissed her cheek. "You alright, hon? You look tired."

"I'm good," she said, placing her tea towel on the rack. "I just got really tired all of a sudden. It's been a long day. It's bedtime for me. Tomorrow will be another busy day with David's mom coming for dinner. I'll figure out in the morning what to make."

She hugged Janessa and asked Jonathan if he was coming up to bed.

"In a bit," He replied. "I want to catch up on the sports highlights. I'll be there shortly."

He knew she would still be awake when he went upstairs. She always read for a while before going to sleep.

Twenty minutes later, when Jonathan went upstairs to their bedroom, Laura was sitting on the bed with a box of papers scattered around her. She had a dazed look on her face and was running her hands through her disheveled hair. She still had her makeup on and hadn't yet undressed. Jonathan closed the bedroom door.

"What's up? What are you doing? You look like you've seen a ghost."

"My God, Jonathan!" She sounded panicky. "Janessa's fiancé is David Bryant, Jr., the son of David Bryant. Remember the guy I told you about twenty-three years ago . . . when I was on a course in Calgary . . . Tyler's birth father? Well, Tyler and Janessa's fiancé are half-brothers!" Her voice broke. "What are we going to do? "

She felt her world crashing. Why hadn't they told Tyler about his biological father? Why hadn't they shared all this information with their children? How did the years pass so quickly and the whole affair get swept under the rug? Did Cathie Bryant know about David's affair? Did she know David Sr. had fathered a child?

This woman who had been so composed and such a strong support to her daughter was now emotionally spinning in circles. When she had left the kitchen for her bedroom, she knew exactly where to look for the information she needed. Deep in the back of her closet lay a small black tin box where she kept sentimental items from years past—special cards her children had given her over the years, memorabilia from her teenage years, and a few other special items. David's obituary from the Calgary Herald, with all the information about his wife and children, was at the bottom of the box. She kept it not out of love but for the day when she would tell her children the story. She had always planned to tell them the truth but, somehow, the years had slipped by, and the story was never told.

Jonathan wrapped his arms around her. "Honey, we'll get through this. I know right now there must be so much going through your mind, but we'll find a way to tell the kids and David's family. Right now, we should focus on David getting better. Our children are engaged, so we'll be one big family before long."

Laura was so grateful for the man she had married. Not only was he handsome and loving, but he always knew how to take care of her and their children. He would make everything right. Held by Jonathan, she felt better and reassured. After they tidied the room and crawled into bed, Jonathan held his wife in his arms and reminded her what a strong and amazing woman she was. How she had overcome so many challenges in her life already. It wasn't long before Laura dozed off—he felt her body relax and her breathing gradually slow. Then he lay awake, wondering how all of this would turn out.

DAVID

David stirred as he slowly woke up in his hospital bed. *Where am I? Why am I hooked up to all these machines?* His brain was also awakening, and memories of the weekend sputtered through his mind. The trip to Diefenbaker Lake, the beautiful drive. He saw himself smiling at Janessa . . . the surprised look on her face when he proposed to her at dinner. She had looked so beautiful in her white linen dress dotted with huge red poppies . . . her eyes were so filled with love . . . the people in the restaurant applauding . . . The way he tenderly loved Janessa that night when they returned to the cottage. He couldn't remember anything after that.

He tried to move around but the wires from the machines prevented him. His head hurt, but the pain that had woken him was in his lower abdomen. He looked around the room then heard footsteps coming down the hallway.

"Mr. Bryant, you're awake!" said the nurse as she approached his bedside. "You've been a sleepyhead for the past few days."

"What happened?"

Before she could answer, Cathie walked into the room.

"Mom?"

Now he was really confused. He hadn't seen his mother for a while.

"Yes, honey, I'm here!"

"What are you doing here?"

Cathie ran to his bed and kissed him. She told him what she had been told about the accident.

"Really? I don't remember much. Have you met Janessa?

"Yes!" she replied. "We've both been here quite a bit. She should be arriving soon."

He twitched in pain from his abdomen. The nurse left to alert the doctor that David was awake. Cathie texted Janessa to let her know the good news, and a few minutes later, she joined them. She had entered the hospital foyer when she received Cathie's text. When she saw David with his eyes open, she rushed to hug him as her emotions overwhelmed her. Tears flowed as they embraced. It had been a long two days of uncertainty, but now she cried tears of gratitude. With the sparkle of the morning sun—at that moment—Cathie saw the diamond ring. She was surprised and disappointed that David hadn't told her about the engagement. She said nothing, unaware their engagement had occurred only hours before the accident.

Dr. Friesen entered the room during the commotion and tears. He addressed David, Cathie, and Janessa, expressing that while David had emerged from the coma on his own, a very good sign of his body healing, he was still concerned about his kidneys. The exploratory later that day would allow them to see what damage had been done. David was not out of the woods yet. He was lucky to be alive and blessed to be surrounded by his family.

"I'll be back to collect David for the exploratory," Dr. Friesen said. "The operating rooms have been extremely busy these past two days due to several vehicle accidents in the city. The nurse will be by shortly with pain meds to keep you comfortable until then, David."

As soon as he left, David, Janessa and Cathie continued talking. The nurse soon appeared with pain medication and removed the heart monitor. The catheter and IV were still required until such time as David was able to get out of bed on his own. Dr. Friesen did not want him moving around too much yet.

Janessa stayed as close to David as she could. She was overjoyed to see him awake. Her face was full of smiles, and her eyes sparkled. They talked about all that had happened since the accident and the days leading up to it. Cathie heard about where and how they met, that they had casually dated for a couple of years but had become more serious only in the past few months. When Cathie left later that morning to call her daughters, she had new peace in her heart.

LAURA

When Janessa returned to her parents' house later that day, her sunny smile told it all, and her mother immediately saw that the prognosis was more positive. When she walked in the front door, her mother hugged her tightly and, together, they cried happy tears.

Janessa had called earlier to tell them David was out of the coma and still had a long way to go, but there had been a huge improvement. She had felt helpless watching him in a coma; now, being able to talk to him was so comforting. Her parents had been thrilled to hear the news. Janessa told her mother the events of the morning. Things were finally looking up.

"I'm kind of nervous about Cathie joining us tonight. She seems so nice. I just hope she feels comfortable with us."

"Future mother-in-law" sounded formal and grown-up. As nervous as Janessa was, she was unaware of her mother's thoughts.

Laura was more than nervous. Her hands were sweaty, and she repeatedly cleared her throat. She and Jonathan had talked extensively about Tyler and David Bryant, Sr., and both agreed it was best not to share anything yet.

"Let's celebrate David's improvement and allow things to unfold as they should," Jonathan said.

Janessa showered and felt more relaxed in her Lululemon loungewear as she helped her mother in the kitchen. The lasagna, a family favourite, smelled scrumptious and went perfectly with homemade Caesar salad and garlic bread. The aroma in the kitchen was mouthwatering. As they worked together, they talked about Janessa moving back to her apartment, making plans for the wedding, and of their gratitude for David's first steps toward recovery.

Cathie arrived at five o'clock, and the Winters family made her feel at home. Jonathan poured the Chardonnay, and they headed to the cozy family room. The late day sun still shone brightly, and the atmosphere was warm and friendly.

"I called my girls to tell them David is awake, and they were so happy to hear." Cathie said.

Janessa had called Tyler and Susie, and both were relieved to hear that David was improving. They hadn't met him yet, but the excitement in her voice told them enough.

Both mothers got to know each other and continued to share stories of their children. Everyone felt relaxed after living with the burden of intense stress.

When Cathie returned to the hotel a few hours after dinner, she felt she had new friends and a new family. They had yet to talk about the engagement and the wedding, but David's recovery came first. Only one thing left her with concern. She had excused herself following dinner to go to the washroom. The wall in the upstairs hallway was filled with family photos, and she had paused to look at them. Many were of Janessa and her siblings at various ages, but it was the photo of a young boy, around six years old, that captivated her.

She assumed the boy was Tyler. There was something eerily familiar about the picture, like she had seen it before. She looked at the other photos but kept coming back to this one before she returned downstairs. She never mentioned the pictures to the family and went back to the hotel soon after.

"Thanks so much for your warm hospitality and the amazing dinner. The meal was better than at any five-star restaurant!" she said.

Laura blushed with pride. She was a superb cook and always found joy in sharing her home and meals.

"Janessa, I'll see you at the hospital tomorrow morning," Cathie said.

The women hugged, and she was on her way.

CATHIE

As Cathie prepared for bed that night, the face of the little boy in the photo stayed with her. She experienced restless sleep, her mind going back to when she had lost her husband years before. Bits and pieces of that troubled time kept resurfacing. She tossed and turned and woke up in a sweat. Why was this picture so familiar? Why was it of such significance to her?

When she walked into David Jr.'s room the next morning, her heart was full. He and Janessa were laughing and having fun—a considerable change from the previous morning. Now that David had stabilized and no future surgery was planned at this point, she decided to return to Calgary for a few days. David would remain in hospital for a few more weeks, and she could drive to Calgary and return to Saskatoon on the weekend. She hoped Anna and Olivia could join her but, next time, they would fly.

She spent a few hours with David and Janessa before getting on the road. She didn't like driving in the dark, especially on unfamiliar roads. Exchanging hugs with her son and future daughter-in-law and promising to text Janessa when she arrived home, Cathie left the hospital after again offering her thanks to Janessa and her parents.

The trip home was long but uneventful. She didn't pay much attention to the scenery this time as her mind reviewed all that had happened. She was relieved with David's recovery progress and excited to tell her girls the good news.

A baby deer jumped out in front of the car, causing her to swerve to avoid hitting the young animal. She was badly shaken, but there was not much traffic on the highway and, after calming herself, she thought it best to let go of the last few days and concentrate more on where she was.

The landscape changed as she drove downhill into the city of Drumheller. There obviously had been lots of rain, and the hills were lush and green. She remembered the first time seeing the Hoodoos, a group of stone columns on some eleven acres of land between Drumheller and East Coulee and having no idea what they were. Fascinating to see and hard to believe that dinosaurs had roamed the area millions of years earlier.

The family had visited when the children were younger and they all had amazing memories of Drumheller. She smiled to herself, remembering how David Jr. made sure to take his sisters by the hand when crossing the street to see the world's largest dinosaur there. He had told her more than once that he had to look out for the girls now that Dad was gone. One of their favourite things was stopping at Dairy Queen after visiting the Royal Tyrrell Museum. David Jr. had loved dinosaur fossils, but the girls were more excited about the ice cream. Just for old time's sake, she pulled into Dairy Queen for a brief rest and a chocolate covered ice cream cone.

It was after seven by the time she arrived home, and Olivia and Anna were having a late supper. She left her bags in the hallway, washed up, and joined them. They had so many questions. How was David doing? Was he going to be okay? Would he need another surgery?

"Hold on a minute!" Cathie said. "Give me a minute to answer before you ask another question!"

She told them about David and Janessa waterskiing and how the accident happened. They grimaced when they heard about the blow to David's head and the commotion that followed with the ambulance ride to the city. They were happy to hear he was conscious now and resting comfortably. She reminded them that although his doctor was pleased with his progress, there still were concerns.

When she had called the girls from Saskatoon after first seeing David Jr., she didn't tell them about the engagement.

"Something else happened before the accident," Cathie said.

Anna waited to see where this would lead.

"Something like what?" Olivia asked.

"There's going to be a wedding! David proposed to Janessa the night before the accident, and she said yes!"

The girls shrieked with excitement. They had never been to a wedding, and the squealing that followed was ear-piercing.

"What's she like? Will we like her? Is she pretty? How old is she? Do you think she'll fit in with our family?"

They were used to an older brother, but an older sister-in-law could be lots of fun, too.

Cathie laughed as she answered their questions. "Yes, Janessa is pretty, petite, and fun to be around. I'm sure you'll both love her! And yes, I think she'll fit in with our family just fine."

Her tone changed when she reminded the girls that David was not fully recovered, and there still was the possibility of surgery. For now, though, they could be grateful that he was recovering.

They couldn't wait to meet Janessa and hoped they wouldn't have to wait too long.

By nine o'clock, Cathie needed to go to bed. Everything, including the drive home, had caught up with her. The next day was Sunday, and she was happy to have a day at home where she could get caught up on laundry and other household duties. She had already texted Janessa to say she had made it home safely. Janessa's response was that David had had a good day and was resting. Cathie also sent a text to Daniel, letting him know she was home.

When Cathie put her head on the pillow, she quickly fell into a deep sleep and dreamed of her husband's death. This time, there were more vivid details: the financial mess he had left her in, trips to the bank, her visit to the safe-deposit box, the picture of the little boy. She woke suddenly. Her brain had stored that picture in her mind through all these years. Sleep was not possible now. She had to get up and find that photo.

Years before, she had given up her safe-deposit box at the bank due to rising service charges and purchased a small safe to store important papers at home. It had been a long time since she had taken out the picture and the receipts. She wasn't even sure why she had kept them but, in the back of her mind, she thought she may someday find the boy.

Her heart raced as she rustled through all the papers in the safe. Her Will, power of attorney, personal directive, birth certificates, immunization cards for herself and her children, and David's death certificate. They were all there. At the bottom of the pile, she found what she was looking for: the envelope holding the receipts and the photo. She took the picture out of the envelope and felt her stomach flip-flop.

Staring at the picture, she saw how much he resembled the photo on the wall at Laura and Jonathan's house. When she flipped the picture over and saw the name, Tyler, she gasped. David's future brother-in-law was indeed his half-brother. Both boys had the same father but different mothers.

Had Laura figured this out? Was Tyler aware that Jonathan Winters was not his birth father? Did Janessa and Susie know? Had Laura shared everything with Jonathan about her affair with Cathie's husband?

Cathie never had shared anything with her children about their having a half-brother. She felt it was one of those deep, dark secrets that was unnecessary for them to know. She had told them all the good things about David—how much he had loved them and how proud he was of each of them, the joy he felt spending time with them. They all were grown now, but she never wanted to destroy the positive image and happy memories of their father. Everyone makes mistakes in their lives, and she had forgiven David a long time ago. Once they heard the news of their father's affair, how would they react? She hoped they would be able to forgive him as she had.

She tucked the picture and the receipts into the envelope and put them back in the safe. All this information needed to be shared with her children and the Winters family. Would this make a difference to the children who were about to be married?

The phone rang early the next morning. Cathie felt as though she had just fallen asleep when she reached over to answer the call.

"Hi, Mrs. Bryant, it's Janessa. I had a call from the hospital a few hours ago, and David has had a setback. I'm at the hospital with my mom and dad now. David's kidneys aren't functioning, and Dr. Friesen wants you to call the hospital as soon as possible. The nurse said she tried calling you, but there was no answer. Are you able to call them right away? They won't give me any details because you're David's next of kin."

Cathie heard the panic in Janessa's voice. "I'll call right away. And I'll call you back as soon as I talk to Dr. Friesen. Janessa—" she said firmly. "David is going to be okay. I'm so grateful you and your parents are with him."

Cathie called the hospital, stating who she was and why she was calling. Dr. Friesen immediately came to the phone.

"Mrs. Bryant, I'm sorry to tell you that David's kidneys are shutting down. We've got him on dialysis to keep them functioning, but this is a temporary fix. He'll need a kidney transplant as soon as we can find a match. How soon are you able to get back to Saskatoon?"

"I can book a flight and be there later today," she said.

"Does David have siblings or relatives who could be a possible match?" Dr. Friesen asked. "It's imperative we don't wait too long before the surgery."

Her world was spinning again. She advised him that she and her two daughters would fly to Saskatoon as soon as she could arrange a flight. She offered up a prayer that one of her girls would be a match for David Jr. Time was of the essence. His life was slowing down much sooner than expected. *God, please keep my David safe until we find him a match.*

She called Janessa and relayed the information from Dr. Friesen. "I'm waking the girls now, and we'll be on the next flight to Saskatoon. We'll be there as soon as we can. Flying time is only about sixty minutes, but we need to arrange work and school. I'll call you as soon as our plans are finalized. Can you or one of your parents pick us up at the airport?"

"Of course we can," Janessa replied. "I'll wait to hear from you."

Cathie woke Anna and Olivia then called Daniel to tell him what was going on. Her emotions were running high, and she continued to silently pray for her son.

LAURA

Her mind was in turmoil. Cathie Bryant was coming back to Saskatoon with her daughters today, and the families would meet at the hospital. She thought she should have them all at her house while they were in town. They would eventually be family. Or would they? How would David feel about his future mother-in-law once he knew that many years before she had had a one-night stand with his now-deceased father? How would her own children feel when they heard the news? Would they forgive her? Maybe they could, but what about Cathie and her children?

What a mess! Why had she not shared all this with Tyler and his sisters years ago? It's not like they wouldn't have accepted it. Blended families were a current norm. Laura shuddered when she thought of telling them. But she had Jonathan, her rock, to help her with all of this. He knew the whole truth and still loved her. Maybe her family and David's family would do the same.

DAVID JR.

Dr. Friesen saw David Jr. on his morning rounds accompanied by two nurses. He regularly came alone or with one nurse, and there was a seriousness about him this morning. David wished Janessa was still in the room, but she had gone to the cafeteria to get some coffee.

"David," the doctor said, "I don't have the best news this morning. Your blood pressure has increased because your kidneys are inflamed. Your kidneys are shutting down, and we are concerned you may go into kidney failure. You're in need of a transplant."

David wasn't shocked to hear this, as he had experienced excruciating pain on his left side the night before. Also, the bag attached to the catheter revealed the passing of blood. Dr. Friesen advised they would need to find a donor match—possibly, one of David's siblings or extended relatives. The testing would need to be done as soon as David's family arrived. Surgery was imminent in order to prevent further complications. He said he had already spoken with Cathie, and she and David's sisters would arrive later that afternoon.

When Dr. Friesen left, David was alone to think about what was to come. What if there was no match? What would the future look like for him and Janessa? It wasn't fair to tie her down to someone so sick. Wedding vows stated, "for better or worse," but they weren't married yet. He loved Janessa but couldn't expect her to commit her life to him with the future so uncertain.

He would find a way to break things off and allow her to find someone else who could give her the life she deserved. Tears trickled from his eyes, but he knew he had to make the right decision.

JANESSA

Mom is acting so weird, Janessa thought as she poured herself a cup of coffee. She had asked her mother a couple of questions, but she had seemed a million miles away. It also was strange to see her distraught about David's mother coming back. They had hit it off well despite all that had happened. Whatever it was, though, she had better get over it. There were wedding plans to be made as soon as David was discharged from the hospital. She looked at her ring and smiled. How it sparkled when the sun shone on it! She was still in awe of her being engaged to marry him. She already had told her roommates about the engagement and his condition improving.

As she sat with her thoughts, she heard the front door open and Tyler's voice.

"Hi, sis!" he said, walking into the kitchen. "How are you doing? How's David doing?"

He draped an arm around Janessa. They were a close family and never afraid of showing love for one another.

"I thought I'd tag along with you to the hospital this morning if that's okay," he said, grinning. "It'll be nice to finally meet my future brother-in-law and see if I wish to give my approval."

Janessa was happy to have Tyler join her. She loved her older brother and didn't get to spend much time with him. Although they lived in the same city, they had a different circle of friends and different interests. Tyler had graduated from college a few years before and currently worked as a laboratory technician at Dynalife Lab. He did shift work, so their time together was usually only during holidays and on special occasions.

"Not sure where Mom and Dad are," Janessa said. "I'd love to have you join me at the hospital. And I know you'll approve of David." Then she added conspiratorially, "Just so you know, Mom's acting strange since I told her David and I are engaged."

"Strange how?" Tyler asked.

"Give me a couple of minutes while I get ready. Coffee is fresh if you want to grab another cup. Banana muffins are in the top cupboard. I'll be down in a few minutes—then I'll tell you everything I know."

CATHIE

Olivia and Anna were excited to see David. They had packed as quickly as they could, and Daniel was there to take them to the airport. The girls were happy that their mother was seeing someone. The memories they had of their father had faded with time, and seeing her happy with Daniel made them happy too. He treated her, along with the girls, with great respect. He also was fun to be around, and the more they saw him, the more confident they were that he and their mother would marry.

While they chatted in the car, Cathie told them of the seriousness of David's condition. Both girls were concerned about David and hoped one of them would be the perfect match. Daniel dropped them off at the departure gate and with a quick hug and kiss to Cathie, he reassured her and the girls that everything would work out.

The airport was relatively quiet, and it didn't take long to check in. Once past security, Anna and Olivia wandered through some of the shops, choosing small gifts to bring David and Janessa. David loved mystery novels, and they found a book by one of his favourite authors, along with Purdy's chocolates. Janessa was harder to choose a gift for, but they knew she would be pleased with whatever they gave her. Anna found a cute summer tote bag with the Calgary Tower on it, and both girls decided this was the perfect gift.

While they browsed, Cathie tried to focus on reading the latest Oprah Magazine. Usually, it was one of her favourites; today, though, she had trouble concentrating. Would one of the girls be a match for a transplant? What if there were no matches? She tried to steer her thoughts toward the joy of planning a wedding.

As they arrived back at the gate, their flight was called. They were excited to board the plane and be on their way. The hour-long trip to Saskatoon was easy enough with the exception of a little turbulence just before they landed. Saskatoon had been experiencing extreme heat after Cathie left the city the day before, and now thunderstorms had settled over the area.

The turbulence left Anna feeling queasy, but Olivia barely noticed it. She sat in the aisle seat and was being pursued by a friendly young man who had struck up a conversation with her as soon as she sat down. He asked if she had ever been to Saskatoon, then told her about the city he called home.

"Did you know Saskatoon is called the city of bridges?"

This was news to her, and he took the time to explain the city was appropriately named due to the eight bridge structures spanning the South Saskatchewan River. He introduced himself as Owen, and he clearly was proud of the information he gave Olivia. They continued chatting until the flight landed then exchanged phone numbers before exiting the plane.

Their baggage didn't take long to collect at the carousel, and they said goodbye to Olivia's new friend.

Laura was waiting for them in the arrivals area, and the women embraced like old friends. Anna and Olivia stood by shyly, waiting to be introduced. The girls connected instantly with David's mother and after a few minutes of small talk, they were on their way to Laura's car.

At the hospital, Janessa anxiously waited to meet David's sisters.

THE FAMILIES MEET

Cathie was uncertain of what to expect when they walked into David's room. With the earlier news about his kidneys failing, she prepared the girls as best she could.

Janessa sat on David's bed, and there was another person in the room with his back to the door.

"Hi, Mom!" David said as he sat up, still hooked to machines. Olivia and Anna ran to hug him. The three siblings were excited to see each other. It had been quite some time since David was in Calgary. Cathie introduced Anna and Olivia to Janessa, then Janessa introduced Tyler. He extended his hand to Cathie, and she did the same. His handshake was firm, as his biological father's had been. She saw a strong resemblance in Tyler's actions and looks. He was so much like his father, reminding her of when she first met David Sr. He was close in age to his future brother-in-law, and they already were teasing each other about Janessa. Tyler joked about what David was letting himself in for. The families connected well, and the laughter in the room took away from the seriousness of their being together.

The nurse on duty notified Dr. Friesen that the family had arrived, and it wasn't long before he joined them. He addressed David and both families, explaining that David's kidneys were not functioning well due to the damage done during the waterskiing accident. One kidney had completely shut down and the other was not functioning well enough to keep him alive for the long term. He would need a transplant, and the biggest challenge was finding a match.

Cathie and the girls had discussed their willingness as potential donors. They had done a bit of research while waiting for Daniel that morning and discovered valuable information. Family members would need testing to see if anyone was a perfect match. It was imperative that the donor be emotionally stable and in good condition physically and financially. Cathie agreed to the cover costs involved. Following surgery, the donor would be given pain medication and agree to tests to ensure their body adjusted to the loss of a kidney. There would also be extensive testing for David's possible rejection of the new kidney.

When Dr. Friesen had gone, the sombre mood didn't last long. Tyler's vibrant personality kept the girls laughing while he told stories of growing up with Janessa and Susie. They couldn't wait to meet Susie later that evening at Laura's home.

Thirty minutes later, Cathie reminded them it was time they check into the hotel to freshen up. Janessa's parents had left the hospital, and the girls wanted to stay longer since they were having so much fun with Tyler, Janessa, and David. Cathie didn't force the issue and said she would check into the hotel herself then meet the others downstairs in forty-five minutes for their ride to the Winters' house. She hugged David and said she would see him in the morning after she was tested and while she waited for the girls to be tested.

David felt reassured to have his mother and sisters with him. A kidney from his mom or one of his sisters would mean he wouldn't have to cancel the engagement. Maybe this was the answer to his prayers. When he and Janessa were married, he not only would have a beautiful wife but also the brother he had always wanted as well as another sister. He was delighted his family had accepted Janessa and her family. There would be so much to learn and share in the coming days.

LAURA

She was nervous and sure someone would know something was up. The nervousness she felt was causing her to sweat. Thankfully she had applied mineral powder to prevent her makeup from running. How much did Cathie know? Should she tell her about Tyler? Jonathan had tried to calm her, suggesting she let things unfold as they should. But Laura wasn't sure about anything.

The drive from the hospital to the Winters' home was filled with laughter. Janessa and Tyler bantered back and forth, teasing each other mercilessly. Cathie and the girls loved how well they got along with each other and felt comfortable in their company. As they pulled in the driveway, Susie came out to greet them.

"Mom's busy taking buns out of the oven, and Dad is getting wine from the basement," she said. "Hi, I'm Susie. You must be Cathie!"

They shook hands, and Cathie introduced Anna and Olivia to her.

"Let's go inside," Susie said. "Mom and Dad are waiting for us."

She was a miniature of Laura. Petite in stature, with blonde hair like her mother, but she was more vivacious, much like Tyler. Janessa was the quietest of the three children but could hold her own with her siblings.

Inside, everyone headed to the kitchen and gathered around the island. Jonathan offered a beverage to everyone, and the families spent time chatting about David. The Winters were a fun family, and Cathie and the girls plainly enjoyed themselves. Only David was missing.

Supper was spent in laughter and reminiscing about the children growing up. There were stories of David becoming the man of the house when his dad died, Tyler and his friends chasing his sister's friends, Anna and Olivia and their days of putting on makeup to look older. They always had a crush on one or all of David's friends. Both girls blushed in embarrassment and denied it vehemently. Everyone laughed like a single family.

The topic of potential wedding dates came up, but Janessa asked that they hold off until David was with them.

Ultimately, David's upcoming surgery was discussed. Anna, Olivia, and Cathie had appointments the following day to see if any one of them might be a match. They each felt unsettled in their own way, but none wanted to show their emotions. The conversation was kept light and hopeful.

The night ended too soon for Anna and Olivia. Despite the reason for coming to Saskatoon, they were having a good time. Everyone pitched in after the outstanding meal of homemade burgers and salads. The best part was Laura's chocolate cheesecake. When she offered seconds, no one refused.

Tyler offered to drive them back to the hotel, as he was heading to the same side of town. There were hugs before they left with promises of seeing Janessa at the hospital the following day. Both families felt hopeful there would be positive news to come.

OLIVIA

She was nervous about being tested the next morning. Secretly, she was extremely worried about David. She loved her brother and when she saw him in his hospital bed, she was frightened for him. She was a young woman who kept her emotions well hidden, unlike her sister, Anna, who openly expressed her feelings.

She said nothing to her mother or Anna but couldn't help wondering what would happen if there were no matches. Would David die, or would he be on a machine for the rest of his life? She tried to put her fears aside as she, Anna, and Cathie prepared for bed.

Tyler entered her mind. He was handsome and funny and definitely knew how to keep a crowd amused. She loved his positive attitude about life—dealing with whatever came about. No big deal. He was loud and outspoken but kind and fun to be around. She hoped she would get to see him the following day after they had all been tested.

As she lay in bed in the dark, thinking of Tyler, she knew she was smitten with him and hoped Anna wasn't interested.

"What do you think of the Winters' family?" she asked her sister.

Cathie was already in bed in the other room. She had booked a suite so the girls could have some privacy.

"Tyler's cute and funny, but not my type," Anna replied. "I prefer someone a little older and more mature."

Olivia breathed a sigh of relief.

"I love Janessa," Anna went on. "Did you see how she looks at David? She's so in love with him. And Susie looks just like her mom. I think Laura and Jonathan are pretty great too."

"Yeah," Olivia agreed warmly.

The room soon became quiet and, before long, both girls were fast asleep.

THE TESTS

Everyone was up bright and early the next morning. Olivia was very selective in her choice of clothes. She wanted to attract Tyler's attention. A tight pair of leggings and a flouncy fuchsia top set off the blue in her eyes. Anna couldn't have cared less about whether she looked good. She went for cute and comfy. After a quick breakfast was delivered, consisting of tea, coffee, orange juice, fruit bowls, and croissants, they all left for the hospital.

The appointments had been booked close together, and the three of them went to the laboratory at the same time. Blood tests were done to see if the potential donor's blood and tissue type matched the transplant candidate. With a match, the donor and candidate would be a "compatible pair." The test results, which usually took a week, were on rush order due to the severity of David's case.

The blood test themselves didn't take long. While each of the girls was being tested, the other was on her phone catching up with friends.

An hour later, Cathie led her girls to David's room to await the results.

They were still at the hospital later that day when Dr. Friesen broke the news to them. The results were not good. There was no match. Now what?

Janessa tried to be as strong for David as he was for her. Dr. Friesen had been the bearer of this type of news to many families, and he gave them a few minutes to absorb what they had heard. He reminded them not to give up hope. They would continue the search until they found a match. Meanwhile, he suggested they allow David time to rest. Tomorrow would be a new day.

LAURA

When Janessa got home and saw her parents, she broke into tears. She had held up a good front at the hospital for David and his family, reinforcing Dr. Friesen's view of it being only a matter of time. David had appeared devastated, as did his mother and siblings. *Someone* had to be optimistic, and Janessa decided it would be her. She told her parents the news, and they held her as she wept.

Seeing Janessa in so much pain convinced Laura of what had to happen next. She had no other choice. As David's half-brother, Tyler might well be the needed match.

When she and Jonathan went to bed that night, they discussed what they should do. Time was of the essence now, and no matter what the outcome, revelations from the past had to be shared however rough on everyone.

Firstly, Cathie Bryant would know her deceased husband had cheated on her—and with Laura Winters the prospective mother-in-law of her son! Would Cathie ever trust Laura again, or would this turn her against her son marrying into Janessa's family?

Secondly, there were Laura's own children. Their mother had had an affair with a married man, and their brother, Tyler, was born out of wedlock. What would they think? There were so many questions that would be asked. She and David Bryant Sr. may have been younger at the time, but would this tarnish her relationship with her children now? Would they look at her differently? Think less of her?

"They will still love you," Jonathan reassured her. "You're a great mom."

Jonathan was her strength, and he was right. They would get through this together.

The best outcome would be that Tyler was a perfect match for David. But how would Tyler feel when he discovered that Jonathan was not his biological dad?

Who should they tell first: Tyler or Cathie? Should they share it with all the children at once or one at a time?

Laura sent a text to Cathie and asked that she come alone for coffee the next morning. Jonathan would pick her up at the hotel at eleven o'clock. He had taken the day off work and would be there to support his wife when she told her story.

CATHIE

When Cathie received Laura's text, she wasn't surprised. Dr. Friesen had given the news that neither she nor the girls were a match for David. She knew the next step: Tyler.

But this meant Laura knew that the boys were half-brothers.

The truth was about to be told and, although Cathie had accepted the fact that her deceased husband had had an affair with Laura so many years ago, she remained unsure how her own children would feel.

Maybe enough time had passed. Her children's memories of their dad were mostly through photos and stories. If Tyler was a match, and this saved her son's life, how could their sisters not forgive David Sr. and Laura? Tomorrow would be an interesting day.

LAURA

Laura felt anxious when she woke up. Her stomach was upset, but this had to be done. Coffee and muffins were ready, and Jonathan reassured her with a hug that it would go well. Many years had passed—fifteen to be exact. Cathie had been on her own for fifteen years. A loved one is never forgotten, but time does heal.

Jonathan left the house at ten-thirty to pick up Cathie. She was waiting for him in the hotel lobby and hurried to his car when he pulled up. Laura was blessed to have such a terrific husband. They chatted idly on the drive back, and Jonathan gave her a tour of the city's most interesting places, the perfect distraction for them both.

When they reached the house, the women embraced like old friends. Laura had coffee and muffins on the table, and the kitchen was warm and inviting, a pleasant atmosphere in which to tell a difficult story.

After catching up on David and there being no suitable match, Laura told Cathie she had something to tell her that was difficult to talk about. She wasted no time.

"I knew your husband, David, many years ago. We met when we were on a course in Calgary. He was such a sweet guy, and I was single, new to engineering, and very timid and shy. He took me under his wing, and we formed a fast bond."

She continued before Cathie could say anything.

"We spent a few days together and, on a couple of evenings, we had supper together."

She lowered her eyes as she disclosed the next part of her story.

"We were young and foolish and careless. After a night of dinner and wine, one thing led to another, and David and I slept together."

Cathie said nothing. She now had her answer. It had been so long ago. How should she respond? Her husband betrayed her, but she knew now it had only been a one-night stand.

"Cathie, nothing more happened between David and me. I never saw him again, but I contacted him months later to advise him I was pregnant, and I knew he was the father. I hadn't been seeing anyone for months before meeting David. Tyler was the gift of our one-night stand. We never saw each other again after the course. When Tyler was born, I contacted David to let him know. We arranged for him to provide child support for Tyler. I periodically sent pictures to David at work but, other than that, we had no contact."

Jonathan reached across table and held his wife's hand.

"I don't know how much David told you, if anything," Laura said. "I'm so sorry for the pain I've caused you and your family."

There were tears in her eyes as she looked at Cathie with deep remorse. The secret was out. As hard as it was, it felt good to have it lifted off her mind.

Cathie waited before she replied, choosing her words carefully.

"We've all made mistakes. Some are revealed and some are hidden. I did know David had an affair, but I didn't find out until after he passed away. I was going through some of his things, and I found Tyler's picture and receipts for child support. At the time, I couldn't understand or make much sense of anything. I'd always hoped I'd eventually be able to figure things out, so I kept the papers tucked away. When I saw Tyler's picture on the wall the first time I was here, I have to admit I was stunned. His picture looked so familiar, but I wasn't sure why at first. It wasn't until I got home and pulled out the photo and papers that I put the pieces together. There were still missing pieces, but now I understand."

Her eyes met Laura's. "I wanted to know why he had done it, why he never told me, but David was gone. I was dealing with grief and looking after my children. I'm sad that David felt he had to go elsewhere looking for love but, back then, maybe he had his reasons. Who knows? We had a great marriage. But like all couples, we had our challenges too. Whatever happened between you and David, I know he loved me, and I loved him. The past is in the past, and I forgave him along time ago."

She sat back and took a Kleenex from her purse to wipe her eyes.

"Thank you, Laura, for being honest enough to tell me the truth. This can't have been easy on you. I want to say I forgive you, too."

A calmness settled over both of them. The long-held secret had been revealed, and a new bond had been formed between the two women.

"Thank you for being so understanding," Laura said.

"Now that all this is finally in the open," Jonathan interjected, "we should tell our children. Tyler always has been my son, and I've never thought anything more about it. David may have fathered him, but I claimed him as my boy many years ago. He *is* my boy, but I hope he may be a match for David's kidney transplant."

Cathie sighed. All these years of not knowing who the little boy in the picture was only to find out he would become her son's brother-in-law and a possible donor match, besides.

Cathie, Laura, and Jonathan hugged each other, grateful for the years that had passed, leaving them able to accept what had happened and move on. All that mattered now was that Tyler might be a match for David.

They called a family meeting the next night at the hospital. The conversation wouldn't be easy, but they hoped the children would accept their parents' past mistakes.

DAVID

The night before at the hospital had felt surreal. David's future brother-in-law was also his half-brother. Both families gathered in his room. They talked about his father, David Sr., his mother, and Laura, his soon-to-be mother-in- law. Both women had a civilized conversation knowing Tyler was the outcome of an affair between his father and Laura.

The siblings had stared at her with disbelief, and there was a heavy silence in the room until Tyler spoke up.

"No matter who fathered me, you're my dad," he said. He went to Jonathan and threw his arms around him.

"From the day your mom and I decided to get married, I saw you as my son," Jonathan replied.

The love between father and son was felt by all in the room. Affairs happen. Children are born out of wedlock.

The room soon buzzed with excitement. There was now a possible donor match, and the families would speak with Dr. Friesen the following day. There was indeed always hope.

TYLER

Never questioning who his father was, Tyler Winters had known for a long time that Jonathan Winters was not his birth father. He had been eight years old when his mother and Jonathan were married. They never talked about his biological father. From the beginning, Johnathan became his real father, the one who took him to hockey practice in the early hours of the morning, the one who attended all his school functions. Jonathan loved Tyler more than life, and that was all that mattered. Tyler had never questioned anything about their family, and he was secure in his mind about who he was and always felt loved. He would now simply have the chance, through David, Olivia, and Anna, to learn more about where he had come from.

As he prepared for the next day's match test, he prayed aloud that he would be a match. The week had been stressful, and they needed some good news. What better news than, as his half-brother, being the right match for David. Then he could recover, and the joy David and Janessa would feel as they planned their wedding would be shared by the whole family. *Both* families.

The results would be known later in the afternoon.

THE REVEAL

They gathered once again in David's hospital room the next afternoon. Dr. Friesen asked them all to be there by three o'clock. The night before, both sets of girls had asked their mothers unending questions. Cathie and Laura had agreed to keep the information at a minimum. All that was needed to be told had been shared. Now it was time to get David's surgery over with so that he and Janessa could plan their life together. The two held hands as the families quietly chatted, hoping for good news.

Everyone fell silent when Dr. Friesen entered. He didn't mince his words.

"I'm so sorry to tell you that Tyler is not a match."

David was the first to speak. "What are my options now?"

Janessa did her best to hold herself together, but tears quickly filled her eyes, and her mother wrapped her arm around her shoulder.

"Are there any other family members?" "

"No," Cathie replied. "My husband had a brother with whom we lost contact years before my husband died. He was the only living relative as far as I know."

"We haven't given up," Dr. Friesen said kindly. "For the next few days, we'll continue to monitor David and make a plan. Where there is faith, there is hope. I'll check back with any news in the next day or so." He nodded and smiled, then quietly left the families to themselves.

No one knew what to say until Laura spoke.

"I agree with Dr. Friesen," she said. "We must not lose hope. There has to be a match somewhere. Let's trust and believe that something good will happen. Look how blessed we are that our families have come together."

They all nodded their heads in agreement and tried to focus on the positive. Cathie changed the conversation to wedding plans. Where did David and Janessa want to get married? Had they thought of a date yet? What colours did Janessa want? Her questions were good distractions for everyone. The afternoon went by, and both families departed at the same time, leaving David to rest. Janessa promised him she would return later in the evening. As she kissed him, she whispered, "God's got this!"

When they exited the hospital, everyone was in better spirits and hopeful that good news would come soon.

Cathie and the girls went shopping for a few hours at Midtown Plaza before boarding an evening flight back to Calgary. No one knew how long a wait there might be before finding a match for David. Janessa thought the mall would be a fun distraction for a few hours for Cathie and the girls. Midtown Plaza had recently opened a Saks and Holt Renfrew, and both stores carried their favourite trendy clothes.

Cathie would return to Saskatoon the following week to see David and continue to commute as necessary. This was a hard waiting game, and nothing more would happen right away. For everyone else, life would have to continue as best as it could.

CATHIE

As planned, Cathie and the girls returned to Calgary later that night. It had been another long week with new discoveries and emotions. She now technically had a stepson who not only would be a brother-in-law to her son but also his half-brother. How can this be explained to people? Now that she knew about the boy in the picture, it wasn't necessary to ask Laura anything more about the affair. David Sr. had been laid to rest, and whatever the reason for the affair was his doing and not hers.

Her relationship with Daniel grew stronger every day, and she could lean on him. She updated him daily and shared the news of Laura and David Sr.'s affair as well as the outcome. What a tangled web! This last trip had made Cathie realize how much she loved and missed Daniel. She didn't want to wait much longer to see him and have him hold her in his arms. She would call him tomorrow and invite him to the house.

She also needed to call Susan who deserved to hear everything after her unwavering support and concern.

Cathie wasn't sure what the future might hold, but she knew who held the future. Her prayers for David that night were filled with anguish. *Please God, find a match for my son. I'm not ready to lose him. I know you're in control, and I trust in you!*

JANESSA

She tossed and turned through the night caught up in dreams. She relived her excitement and David's proposal during dinner. They went waterskiing the next day, and she lost her engagement ring. David was furious that she would be stupid enough to wear the ring in the water. She had never seen this side of him. A loud buzzing came from the boat's motor. She woke to the sound of her phone ringing. It was eight a.m., one week since Dr. Friesen had revealed that Tyler was not a donor match. She sat up and answered her phone.

"Janessa? This is Dr. Friesen from St. Paul's Hospital. We found a match for David!"

He didn't give further details but only that surgery would begin in four hours.

"Could you contact David's family then come to the hospital by nine-thirty? I'm sure you want to be present when we tell David the news."

"I'll be there!" she replied, almost screaming the words.

She was wide awake now and grateful they had put her name on David's chart as next of kin. Both she and Cathie thought this was best. She raced downstairs.

"Mom! Dad! Oh my God! They have a match for David!"

Laura and Jonathan were having coffee together.

"I can't believe it! Mom, can you call Cathie? I want to be at the hospital by nine-thirty when they tell David. Please tell Cathie, David and I will call her as soon as we hear more. Oh my, God is so good!"

She raced to hug her parents. She wasn't sure how all of this came to be, but prayers were being answered.

CATHIE

She answered the phone as she prepared her lunch to take to work. She was surprised to hear the excitement in Laura's voice.

"Cathie, they've found a match for David!"

"Really? Thank God!" Cathie said.

She had been so concerned about David that she had woken several times during the night and prayed.

"I don't have any more details," Laura said, "only that they found a match. Janessa is heading to the hospital right now and will be with David when Dr. Friesen tells him the good news. She'll call you as soon as they have more details. Prayers have been answered, Cathie! I'm so grateful this is all going to work out!"

"Me too!" Cathie exclaimed. "Me too!"

DAVID

He was surprised to see Janessa at the hospital so early in the morning. Maybe now, when it was just the two of them, would be a good time for him to break off the engagement. He had been pondering this for several days since they found out that Tyler was not a match. Then he thought, *What if something's gone wrong?*

She saw the anguish on his face and kissed him, telling him to relax. She knew of his fears but knew that, together, they would see it through.

Dr. Friesen walked in with a wide smile on his face.

"Good news!" he said to David. "We have a match!"

The stress had held David's emotions tightly inside him, but now he cried before Dr. Friesen had even finished telling him the details. He was young and had everything to live for. With a new kidney, he would have a new lease on life. His future wife was beside him, and he loved her and wanted to spend the rest of his life with her—now he had the chance to do so. Now the dam broke. All his hidden emotions about his father, Laura, and Tyler bubbled up. All he had held back poured out. Janessa held him like a baby and let him cry it out.

Dr. Friesen did not reveal details of where the kidney was coming from—only that David would be in surgery by two o'clock that day. He and Janessa were ecstatic. When Dr. Friesen left them, they called Cathie, then Laura and Jonathan. Cathie would be on the earliest flight she could book to Saskatoon.

Things began happening quickly. David would be prepped for surgery by noon. Laura was on her way and she and Jonathan would be with their daughter while David was in surgery. Dr. Friesen said it would take some four to six hours, and David would be in recovery for an hour. They would be able to see him by nine o'clock that night.

David and Janessa emotionally prepared themselves, and they talked about all that had happened in the last while. They knew how much they loved each other, and the road ahead would not always be easy, but as husband and wife, they would face the challenges together.

CATHIE

It had been six weeks since David's surgery. Both families were gathered in celebration at Laura and Jonathan's house: Cathie and Daniel, David and Janessa, Laura and Jonathan, Anna, Olivia, Susie, and Tyler.

They had recently learned that the kidney David received was from a twenty-year-old man who had been tragically killed in a car accident. He had signed his donor card the previous year, and David was the lucky recipient of a healthy kidney. Cathie felt sad for the young man's family but so blessed that David could be the recipient. Her son was able to live because someone else's son had died, not something easy to understand. Life must be lived forward and understood backwards. A time to be born and a time to die.

Cathie's faith had been growing in the past few years. It had been tested many times with the passing of her husband at a young age. But she was learning about God, who He was, and how much He loved her. Life was confusing at times, especially with so much hurt and pain in the world, but she was learning to trust and believe.

As she glanced around the yard and saw the people who were there, laughing and having fun, she raised her eyes to heaven with a smile of gratitude. Through all the unfair twists and turns, Cathie found strength, and, through faith, there is hope. Kindness and forgiveness go a long way. And the truth will always set you free!

Blessings come in many disguises, and Cathie and her family were truly blessed.